How to Master Moonshine

Index

How to Master Moonshine

By R.W. Marshall

Disclaimer

This is a book for informational purposes only.

I hope you enjoy reading the information and techniques contained in this book, but before actually using any of the methods described, you should check into the laws of your country and region to see what is allowed as far as producing any kind of alcohol. Different countries, provinces, states and regions have different rules.

Some countries do allow the legal distillation of spirits for personal use while others have restrictions requiring permits. If you live in one of those countries, such as New Zealand, Italy, Russia and Ukraine, this guide will help you learn step by step how to get the best results.

For others, this book is for information only, and if you use it for anything else, it is at your risk. In no way do I condone breaking any laws in your particular area.

Despite the tongue-in-cheek cover, which is really a caricature on the history of moonshine, what I offer here are safe methods and recipes for making your own alcohol, liquors and liqueurs.

If you are under the legal drinking age of your country, do not make or consume alcohol.

Whatever you do with the information in this book, it is YOUR responsibility to ensure that you do so safely and with full knowledge of what you are doing.

You, the reader and or user of this information, may not hold the author their distributors or agents liable for any misfortunes that you encounter, or legal consequences of your actions. You must fully educate yourself before undertaking anything written or implied in this book. If you have any doubts about your abilities, equipment, methods, ingredients to use, or the legal consequences, do not attempt it. Seek further help if necessary before undertaking any actions.

By acting on any information contained in this book you the reader and or user of this information acknowledge that you understand the dangers involved and agree to indemnify and hold harmless the author, distributors and agents from and against all claims, damages, losses, bodily injury, or property damage arising from your actions, errors or omissions.

I should also note that in nearly every country, it is illegal to SELL your alcohol without proper licensing procedures. Even if it is legal to make wine for instance, you may only make it for your personal use, not to sell. If you want to sell it, go through the proper government approved process to obtain permits and commercial license(s).

The techniques in this book will show you how to make large quantities of alcohol. Please, do not drink to excess. Large amounts of alcohol can be deadly, especially if consumed in conjunction with other drinks such as 'energy drinks', high caffeine-containing beverages, or other drugs for that matter. Know your limits, know what alcohol levels are legally allowed, and don't over-indulge, or use drugs.

The purpose of this book is not to encourage substance abuse, but to allow you the knowledge to produce alcohol safely, and also to encourage sober, intentional thought before consuming it.

You can have a lot of fun with the information you'll get here, but use it safely and carefully.

Please review the laws in your country and act accordingly.

Forward and cautions:

I am writing this book partly because there is a lot of really bad information on the Internet about making moonshine. I think part of the problem of why distilling is illegal, is that you get a lot of uninformed people 'winging it', trying their best to do it themselves, without a lot of understanding, thought to safety, or research into proper techniques.

To write this book, I did a lot of internet research, and was appalled by some of the suggestions, including use of old radiators; using propane burners indoors (on wood floors none the less!); and utilizing many other questionable materials and methods. I watched a lot of videos online, and some were absolutely scary. One person even advocated using grass clippings! I for one would not want to taste his moonshine!

There were also instructions on making your own stills from a wide variety of things ranging from a tea-kettle, to a crock pot, garbage bin, pressure cooker or a beer keg. While some of these things may work, some are just downright dangerous! Please, be very cautious about using any of that questionable advice…stop and think it through. Throughout this book, I will stress safety, cleanliness and common sense in my approach; much as you would when preparing anything that you will be eating or drinking!

I also include lots of recipes for making liqueurs and flavoured spirits with your moonshine. Even if producing alcohol is illegal where you live, <u>you can still use these recipes</u> to legally make these drinks in most countries, by using commercially available grain alcohol and flavourings.

The first thing and last thing I will stress throughout this book is safety. You must understand everything about the process and the steps necessary to produce a good end product, so please read and understand everything.

As the old adage goes: garbage in, garbage out. You must use good quality ingredients and only food-grade materials and edible flavourings. You can make alcohol many different ways, out of many things, but if you wouldn't eat it, or put it in your mouth, why would you want to drink it?

You will learn to safely and effectively produce *ethyl alcohol or ethanol,* which is the kind of alcohol in every kind of beer, wine or spirit on the market. It is also the only SAFE type of alcohol for consumption.

NEVER drink or distil anything containing *methyl alcohol, rubbing alcohol, ethylene glycol, or isopropyl alcohol,* or others which are found in a variety of **non-consumable** products on the market, such as cleaning products or automotive anti-freeze. Also, *denatured alcohol* is NOT drinkable. It can contain dangerous amounts of methyl alcohol or other additives put in to discourage consumption. Drinking **any** alcohol other than ethyl alcohol can have disastrous consequences such as blindness, or even death. There have been documented cases of people dying from drinking windshield washer fluid, anti-freeze or methyl alcohol. Such a risk is foolhardy and stupid. Do not drink anything you are uncertain about! Also, consuming excess amounts of any drinkable, ethanol based liquor can also lead to death from alcohol poisoning. Too much of a good thing isn't good either.

PLEASE, exercise caution and good sense with both production and consumption. And, NEVER EVER drink and drive...let's keep everyone else safe too! If you're going to drink & party, do so at home and keep it at home; use a designated driver; or stay put for the night! Don't risk anyone's life, including your own.

If you decide to make and distill alcohol, please be sober when you do so. As with anything else, being impaired will often result in mistakes, which usually doesn't have a good outcome for you or anyone else!

And, I take no responsibility for your errors, bad judgement or any consequences that may result from you or anyone else taking action on the information contained in this book.

In this book, you will learn how to make a basic 'wash', which is to say, the combination of ingredients resulting in fermentation, a natural process by which alcohol is made. This can be accomplished using inexpensive sugar and yeast.

Producing alcohol for moonshine is basically the same as that for producing wine, which is legal to make in many countries (note that some countries may require you to add fruit to your wash to be called 'wine'). It is also legal in many countries to *own* a still. After all, you can use it to distil water, vinegar and perfumes, besides the obvious use for alcohol.

The 'illegal' part comes from the act of concentrating or separating the alcohol from the 'wash', which is also sometimes called 'beer' or 'must'. Most governments have strict controls on doing this, mostly *I believe*, because they get large revenues derived from the taxes they charge on alcohol…hundreds of percent in some cases. It's a cash cow that they don't readily want to give up.

You *could* use these methods to remove the alcohol from *wine*, but there are more economical ways to attain basic *ethanol*, the consumable form of alcohol. Wine making usually involves the use of fruit, most commonly grapes, which are high in sugar. Whatever fruit is used will give some flavour of that fruit to the wine. However, wine is more costly to produce and depends on this flavour in the end product. In making moonshine, we are simply after a basic alcohol, and not necessarily a particular flavour.

You will learn methods to extract alcohol from the wash, concentrating it, purifying it, and giving you a 'base' to make whatever spirits you wish.

I will also provide information and recipes on producing various liqueurs and spirits from commercially sold alcohol available at government-approved retailers. This is legal, since you are buying the base alcohol at a recognized commercial source, which already has government taxes applied, and simply using it to create other cocktails, liqueurs and drinks.

I also include links in the Appendix to trustworthy, reliable sources of ingredients. Please don't go out in the woods to gather these yourself unless you know what you are doing!!

Dedication:

I dedicate this book to my Grandfather Oscar and my Uncle Ed, both of whom were moonshiners, and (not so legally), in the privacy of their own homes, distilled alcohol for their own enjoyment, (not to sell or bootleg…).

They came from Europe looking for a better life in a new country at the turn of the last century and lived through the depression, where necessity was the mother of invention.

They succeeded in raising families, feeding them and while not living a lavish lifestyle, enjoying what they had and passing that love of life on to their children.

With wars and the disastrous economy, they could barely afford to feed their families, never mind afford to purchase spirits. They also lived in a rural area, miles from anywhere. And so, took the matter into their own hands and learned to make their own spirits.

Although my relatives technically broke the law making their own liquor, they largely did so out of financial necessity, and I applaud their ingenuity in developing the ability to do so. They both lived long lives, so obviously weren't poisoned in the process! As you will learn, done correctly, there is virtually no chance of poisoning yourself with the alcohol you will make (unless you consume too much!).

That said, I again stress that you should first look into the laws of whatever country you live in. I certainly don't advocate breaking the law, and you should be aware that many countries have severe penalties for doing so.

A bit of history

Although opinions vary greatly about the actual origins of distillation, production of alcohol can be traced back to 7000 BC in ancient China, where they fermented rice and fruit. Alcohol production is present throughout history in virtually every country and most cultures.

Many times, fruit or grains were used to produce crude wine and beer. Concentration of these crude brews through distillation probably began with 'Alembic Distillation'. A very old technique, it was used by the Chinese 3000 years BC, followed by the East Indians 2500 years BC, the Egyptians 2000 years BC, the Greeks 1000 years BC, and the Romans 200 years BC. All of the above cultures produced a liquid, later called alcohol.

Ethanol has been used as a medicinal treatment, and was a common ingredient in many concoctions, elixirs and 'snake-oil' sold by travelling hucksters. However, even today ethyl alcohol forms the base of many medicinal herbal tinctures or extracts. It's even used in mouthwash, motor fuel, hand sanitizer, perfumes and after-shave (but please don't drink these either, since they contain other non-edible ingredients besides alcohol).

Of course, various areas of the world have become known for different spirits. Scotland for scotch, the Caribbean for rum, Russia for vodka, Mexico for tequila, Germany for schnapps, Greece for ouzo, Japan for sake, America for bourbon, Canada for rye whiskey, and so on.

In North America, whiskey was first produced in the mid 1700's. Historically "moonshine" is liquor produced in the dark forests, basements and out of the way places where the government can't reach in and tax its production. People have always had an infatuation with this backwoods brew, which has a long history.

In the United States of America, president George Washington first tried to tax liquor in the late 1700's. This was not met with much support, and was eventually repealed in 1803. Ironically, George Washington himself owned and ran one of the largest distilleries in America at the time! I include his whiskey recipe later in the book. The tax was reintroduced after the War of 1812, and Americans again weren't pleased when they were told they would have to pay an excise tax on whiskey and spirits. After all, they won the war, and why should they be subjected to oppressive British taxation! Scottish-Irish immigrants, armed with the knowledge of how to make whiskey were some of the first to move into the remote mountains of Eastern Tennessee to produce 'shine' by the light of the moon.

Although the government again abandoned this excise tax on liquor in 1817, it didn't slow production of corn mash whiskey, which by then had become firmly entrenched in society. Through the 1800's, battles between government revenue agents and moonshiners escalated with stories and legends made on both sides of the law. Revenuers raided homes and bullied the public into revealing the location of hidden stills and their operators. The people living in the Appalachian Mountains in eastern Tennessee, as well as Southern Kentucky and North Carolina, had become legend in their reputation for defying revenue laws.

When prohibition was enacted in the 1920's (the Temperance movement in Canada), it turned out to be the best thing that could have happened for moonshiners. Suddenly, 'legal alcohol' was not to be found (except by doctor's prescription for 'medicinal need' ☺). The added demand for moonshine rose so quickly, that producers began making it from sugar, as well as other cheap ingredients to increase their production and profit, since it could be produced faster than the traditional 'corn-mash'. During this period, 'runners' delivered the shine to covert distributors, and became legendary for using fast, modern automobiles to outrun lawmen. Unfortunately, it also led to shoddy production habits, with producers using low quality equipment and materials, including radiators containing lead and water from creeks and streams. This led to some people getting sick and even dying, which of course gave moonshine a bad reputation.

When prohibition was repealed in 1933, moonshining became less prevalent, since legal (and safer) spirits could be produced and purchased nearly as cheaply as moonshine. With the legalization of make-your-own homebrew beer and wine in the 1970s, moonshining became less a necessity and more of a hobby. However, the legend of these 'red-neck' defiant mountain men and women continues to fascinate the world.

From this period, many movies and television shows were spawned, glorifying moonshiners and the runners that helped bring it to the public. Such movies as Thunder Road, a 1958 film starring Robert Mitchum; The Last American Hero (1973) starring Jeff Bridges; and Burt Reynolds as a beer bootlegger in Smokey and the Bandit are some of the memorable ones. On television, one of the best-known and best-loved series was 'The Dukes of Hazard' with their supercharged sports car tearing a strip through the back hills. The series also spawned a movie take-off in 2005. Eddie Murphy and Martin Lawrence played two New York City men caught up in a murder while picking up moonshine in Mississippi in the movie 'Life'.

More recently, a number of reality television shows have cropped up, including 'Moonshiners' on the United States Discovery Channel, 'Tickle', even the 'Hatfields and McCoys' which features the original feuding families joining together to make traditional moonshine. These shows have become very popular and have candidly brought the world of modern moonshiners into the living rooms of viewers. They depict how the practice survives today through the lives of a few actual moonshiners making and selling 'shine'.

Some of these moonshiners have 'gone legit' and are now brewing and selling their moonshine legally, but for the most part, it is obvious that there are still many, many illegal operations in place. And, despite being illegal in the US, it is still popular, successful, and profitable especially in the southern states. To provide balance, the shows also present police officers in their efforts to apprehend the makers and sellers of moonshine.

For those fans of the show, let me say that I would not support breaking the law by producing and selling moonshine illegally. Further, the methods they use seem, to some degree, to be risky and unsafe. They use old wood and metal fermentation vats, large tanks of propane in a less than controlled environment, use creek water for the base of production and questionable cleanliness as far as fermentation goes. This all serves to perpetuate the perception that making and consuming moonshine will harm you, and maybe some of this stuff would. Despite this, they are carrying on a long tradition, in many cases passed down from generation to generation, and the romantic mindset people have about the history and black market 'bad-boy' image continues to make it popular. It is much more preferable to follow proper cleanliness, known ingredients (such as clean water), etc.

Keep reading, and you too will know how to do it correctly.

The Basics

I will assume here that you have no experience in producing alcohol or wine in any form. If you are an experienced wine-maker, bear with me...you'll still learn something, even if you're familiar with the basic principles.

Producing alcohol is a fairly easy process. It involves the interaction of yeast and sugar. Yeast loves sugar and readily consumes it. With the addition of some nutrients to feed the yeast, the microscopic organisms will happily munch away on the sugar, producing alcohol in the process.

As someone once pointed out to me, in layman's terms, alcohol is basically yeast 'pee'. Alcohol is a bi-product of the yeast eating the sugar. They 'fart out' carbon dioxide, and 'pee out' alcohol.

If that doesn't gross you out, read on!

In winemaking, fermentation goes through two stages, aerobic, and anaerobic.

Aerobic basically means 'with air'. Anaerobic means 'without air'.

For the first 'aerobic' stage, you start the fermentation in a large bucket, exposing the fruit (mash), sugar and yeast to the air. This provides lots of oxygen for the yeast to breathe and produce alcohol quite quickly. In making moonshine, you only need sugar and yeast. The fruit adds no flavour unless you are making a flavoured brandy with a pot still (more on this later). For now, suffice it to say we will use sugar and yeast.

In wine making, the process then goes through a second stage, which is anaerobic. This is a much slower, more subdued fermentation that can last a few weeks to a few months, depending on the yeast, juice (or must) and overall conditions. This is usually done in a glass carboy, which allows you to see the activity, and protects the wine from air and in some cases light (red wines are more susceptible to light damage). You can use this second stage fermentation for moonshine also, you just don't need to. It would yield a minimal additional amount of ethanol, and would just take longer.

In winemaking, much of the flavour is formed between the slurry of fruit, juice and yeast and how it ferments together for weeks and months at a time. It mellows and changes as it ages, and develops a character, which oenophiles (wine-lovers) take pleasure in dissecting and writing about.

Now, don't get me wrong, I love wine making. In fact, I have been making wine for many years and have won lots of awards for my wines. I'm just stressing that it takes much longer to make a good wine than it will to produce moonshine, ethanol, hooch or whatever lingo you want to use!

Making wine from scratch (picking the fruit, mashing, fermenting, aging and bottling it) can take from 3 months to over a year to produce a nice result. You have to allow the yeast to finish fermenting, clear, then age the wine to 'soften' the flavour and remove some of the bitterness that sometimes comes with a young wine. It's more of an art form to produce a polished product that will be at home on your dinner table.

Don't worry, it won't take months to produce ethyl alcohol for distillation.

Making alcohol intended for distillation only requires the first stage of fermentation, the aerobic stage.

We are only aiming to make the maximum amount of alcohol as quickly as possible. We don't have to worry about the same things as in winemaking. You just don't need that long process in order to produce pure ethanol. As a matter of fact, you can do it in a week or less.

Now, that's not to say that aging won't produce a better result. It certainly will, and depending on the type of distillation you choose, you may age your spirits for years in order to achieve a particular flavour. It's just that you don't *need* to. There are short cuts you can take to produce a perfectly acceptable spirit in days or weeks instead of months or years.

Traditional spirits are made from a variety of substances, ranging from sugar, which we will use here, to sugar cane, corn and other grains, potatoes, and fruit. Each liquor requires its own special treatment, and is often distilled using completely different equipment and methods. There is so much variety of materials and methods that it would be totally impractical for the hobbyist to attempt duplicating what is commercially available. We can however come close by using flavourings and ingredients that will impart the proper tastes and aromas.

In fact, you can produce a scotch that friends would have difficulty telling the difference between yours (done in 2-3 weeks) and an aged scotch from the liquor store.

You will find that your moonshine will be clear as water coming out of the still. In fact, the amber colouring and flavour for whiskeys and other spirits comes from the charred barrels (usually oak), which are used for aging the spirits sometimes for many years before bottling.

Another thing you should know is that if you follow the directions I give, you will NOT produce alcohol that will poison you. If you use food grade materials, sugar and clean water…no toxic amounts of poisons will result. This is a myth perpetuated by authorities to discourage people from doing it themselves. Common sense tells you that sugar, water, yeast…all natural things you eat daily in bread…won't kill you!!

Please note that for measurements, I try to give amounts in cups and litres, but because of different measures in different countries, I use a 'metric cup', which is 250 ml.

A quick word on terms you will read. I described what you start with as a 'wash'. You will also read the terms 'mash' and 'must'. The difference is this…a 'mash' contains solids such as corn or grain used to produce alcohol. 'Must' usually refers to fruit based fermentations. Once these solids are strained out or removed, what you have left is a 'wash'…or liquid that has been fermented, that contains alcohol.

Ingredients

OK, so here we go! Basically, you need cheap sugar (use whatever cane sugar is on sale at the time), a quality yeast (one made for distilling is preferred), a bit of yeast nutrient to feed the little beasties, and some basic equipment. I would recommend at some point you may wish to add more advanced

extraction equipment (such as a still), but you don't need to in the beginning. If you want to use a more expensive sugar such as dextrose, corn sugar, etc., you can. It provides a little easier fermentation for the yeast, (and I use it for winemaking), but for moonshining, the end result will be more or less the same, so there's no need to use more expensive sugar, unless you are fermenting a specific flavour that you will pot distill. More on that later.

I will go into yeast varieties in more detail later, but you *will* need a quality yeast made for wine or specifically for distilling. Please don't run out and buy bakers or brewer's yeast. Although the name suggests it, it really isn't made for brewing as far as our purposes.

Yeast nutrient will either be part of the yeast package you buy, or you may buy it separately online or from a wine or you-brew store.

It's as simple as that. No exotic ingredients, nothing complicated. It can get more complicated if you choose to do a traditional moonshine using grains, but I'll get into that later. For now, this is the best way to learn the basics quickly and easily.

Equipment you need

There is some basic equipment you need to produce any kind of alcohol.

Fermentation bucket & stir spoon

For your wash, you will need a <u>food-grade</u> white or clear bucket large enough to hold a little more than the batch of alcohol you intend to make. I say larger since you need to leave room for some activity that the yeast will produce (a head, foaming etc.). Since the usual batch is 23 litres, use a bucket that holds at least 25 or 30 litres. However, if your still is smaller, you can downsize your batch, or simply distil it in a couple of runs.

You can use a large plastic 'garbage container' style bucket (white or clear). These will be available at a wine supply store, or maybe even at a hardware store. Don't use a coloured bucket, since the colour may not be stable and the colour (or worse the taste) may leach into your wash. Bad, bad, bad. Remember, food-grade.

And, VERY IMPORTANT…no metal. DO NOT use a metal container to ferment in, unless it is <u>food-grade</u> stainless steel or copper. A metal garbage container is NOT acceptable for alcohol production. There are often coatings on these containers, and there is too much contact with the metal for too long during the fermentation process. The metal in these containers isn't stable enough for consumption, and can leach into the wine or wash, producing off flavours and adding unwanted metals into the wash. That can't be good for you. Remember, you're going to drink this stuff!

Always stress SAFETY when producing anything you will consume. If you wouldn't eat a meal off it, why would you use it to produce something you will drink!?!

You could also use a plastic bucket from a 'you brew it' or wine store. They sell wine concentrates in them for brew-it-yourself customers, and go through many dozens of such containers in a week.

However, you might prefer a larger container, since these concentrate buckets are themselves only about 23 litres, and don't leave much room for the yeast to ferment. The solution would be to do a slightly smaller batch, or ferment it in two containers. Then you can certainly use these buckets, and a wine store may even give them to you since they go through so many.

If you are using a commercial still, then make the size of your batch to fit the still. No sense making a 23 litre batch if your still only holds 20 litres!

You will need a stir-stick to mix the sugar and stir the wash (I will refer to the sugar-water combination as 'wash'). A large wooden, plastic or food-grade stainless steel spoon is fine, it just has to be long enough to reach the bottom of the bucket without getting your hands into it. Please clean it each time before stirring.

Find a clean cloth large enough to cover the bucket, and string or elastic to secure it. Bugs love the smell of fermenting alcohol, and it's the last thing you want to see floating in your bucket. It has to be a tight enough weave to keep out even the smallest bugs (fruit flies for example).

You will need some plastic tubing for siphoning the wash into the still, or whatever you are using to extract the alcohol. You can get this tube at any brew, wine or hardware store. Again, use food grade, don't use neoprene!

Once you have extracted the alcohol from the wash, you may wish to purify it even further for flavour purposes. In alcohol production, there are 'levels' of alcohols (called congeners), *some* of which are impurities, and can give various flavours, both wanted and unwanted to the distillate. Although not all of these are good (they won't harm you as a rule, but may not taste the best), some are necessary to impart the characteristic flavour if you are making traditional alcohol such as rum or whiskey.

These congeners have slightly different evaporation or boiling points, and I'll cover how to minimize this later. Controlling these congeners partly depends on the sugar you use, and what yeast you use, since some yeasts impart more of a flavour than others. It also depends how well you extract the alcohol and treat the wash, but again, more about this later. Suffice it to say for now that you may get some off-flavours. To remedy this, you may wish to use activated carbon to filter with after extracting the alcohol. Running the liquor through carbon helps remove these flavours, much as a water filter can help purify the flavour of tap water.

You can buy commercial carbon filters, but it can be expensive. I will give you a design to build your own that isn't too costly. This step is totally optional, and won't affect the drinkability of the moonshine. And, as I said, using yeast that minimizes these flavours may be enough for you.

Besides the equipment for making the wash, you will want to have a few other items on hand.

One is a small glass tube called an alcoholmeter. This will float in your finished alcohol and tell you how much alcohol by volume you have simply by looking at the scale on the tube. I will cover more on that in the chapter on calculating alcohol volume. For that matter, you can also check how much alcohol was produced in your wash before you distil it. That is good to know, especially to check how efficiently your yeast worked to produce the level of alcohol you were expecting.

And of course, you may want to obtain a still to strip the alcohol out of your wash. Not necessarily required, but certainly the most efficient way to get the most out of your wash. More about stills in the next chapter.

The Still

One of the most important pieces of equipment you need is of course a still. While you can make these yourself if you have metal working abilities, most of us don't. Fortunately, there are commercial models available, which you can mail order.

It is legal to own a still in most countries, since it can be used to distil water for example, but you should check the legality of it before investing money and ordering one.

My recommendation would be one made of food grade stainless steel. These are safe to use, and don't tarnish like copper will. Cleanup is easy and they will last virtually a lifetime. I list some sources in the appendix for obtaining these units. The disadvantage with stainless steel is that it doesn't conduct heat quite as well. Copper also helps remove esters and other undesirable compounds from the alcohol vapour. However, this can also be achieved by using copper packing in the stainless steel column. In any case, I'd only use <u>stainless</u> steel or copper.

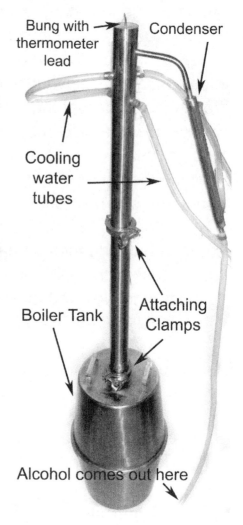

Bung with thermometer lead

Condenser

Cooling water tubes

Boiler Tank

Attaching Clamps

Alcohol comes out here

still set-up

If you do want to make your own still, be sure you know what you are doing. Weld with the proper material, and if you are soldering, use lead free solder, which is available in hardware or plumbing stores. You can buy sheet metal from a metal fabrication company. You may also be tempted to use something like a stainless steel milk can or pressurized beer container. These *are* made to withstand some pressure and banging around, but *aren't* really made for heating. Therefore, over time, faults can develop from the stress of being heated over and over. Also, modifying it for a column will be tricky. You don't want the top blowing off during a run…that would be bad! I take no responsibility for any improvised creation you may make!

Just be aware that there are internal pressures involved when heating alcohol to the boiling point, so SAFETY FIRST!! Don't think you're going to hold the top on with paper clips (seen it on the internet!!), put a rock on top to weigh it down (seen that too), or stuff dough into cracks that develop (yup…that too). It's crazy the chances some people take!

If you do want to make your own still, I include some sources and links in the appendix at the end of the book. It will require some mechanical and fabrication skills, because you are attaching metal pieces to each other. Be sure you have these skills and are confident you know what you are doing. Again, do not use solder or welding materials containing lead. Silver solder, lead free solder, or stainless steel welding is required.

If you do want a proper still, I recommend buying one specifically made for that use. Properly cared for, it will last decades, and you will recoup the cost quickly in what you save in buying alcohol.

If you still want to make your own still, the easiest material to work with will be copper (unless you know how to weld stainless steel). Copper is a better conductor of heat, and it can be soldered rather than welded. Be sure to use no-lead solder. The larger the still, the thicker your copper should be. For a smaller still of about 10 gallons, you can probably get away with 16 oz or 24 gauge copper. For larger kettles it probably isn't practical to make your own, since they would require much thicker copper for the kettle, that would be difficult to work with for the home builder. Plus, that size still would require a fair bit of space, and will be impossible to move once filled! You can often find rolls or sheets of copper at a roofing supplier or from a mail-order company specializing in sheets metals.

If you are looking for a large still, you will need some kind of stand to hold the weight of the still and all of the wash that goes in it. A 'home-size' still will be fine on a stove or hotplate, but larger ones will need a sturdy stand and their own heat source. Please…don't build a stand out of wood…it could burn! Use strong enough steel to support the weight you need.

You should also be sure to have some kind of a thermometer attached to your still. Depending on the model, it may come with this. If not, you can put one on the kettle, or the top of the column. I think it is more useful at the top of the column, since that is where the distillate will begin running. As the alcohol begins to boil, heat increases toward the top, the thermometer then can give you an indication when the run is about to start. If it's on the kettle that will just tell you what the temperature in the pot is.

All of that said, I will also show you how you can get ethanol without even needing a still. More on that later.

An old still, copper all corroded
(don't use something like this!)

Old pot still with coiled condenser

commercial reflux still

Of the above two old pot stills, the centre design isn't bad, but could use a larger 'cap', and the copper tubing and the worm should really be longer, or even better, use a condenser. The left one may have done the job, but I wouldn't recommend this type of homemade contraption! The right picture is a commercial reflux still operation and a good example of what would be used in an artisan distillery (definitely not a home operation!). The column has a series of ports or windows, which allows the distiller to monitor the reflux operation (how far up the column the alcohol is boiling, and therefore gauge how active the process is).

Making a basic wash

A basic wash consists simply of water, sugar, yeast and nutrient. The yeast used will largely determine the quantity of alcohol you end up with. Some types of yeast won't tolerate the presence of higher alcohol and will die out before achieving a decent content. You want as much alcohol as possible for you to extract! There is no sense leaving sugar unfermented in the bucket. So, use an alcohol-tolerant yeast to ferment all the sugar in solution. Resist the urge to use baker's yeast. Many internet recipes call for it, but it really isn't made for this, and it won't ferment to a high content.

I recommend turbo yeasts, which will ferment up to 23 percent alcohol, which by brewing standards is very high. These products may be purchased online (see the appendix for some sources), and cost a bit more than a standard packet of wine yeast. But, they also come with their own nutrient in the packet, so you save a bit of cost that way also. To save a few dollars, you may also use a champagne (Lavlin EC-1118) or port yeast, which will also give a higher alcohol yield (generally 15 to 18 percent). But, they're slower to ferment, and you will need to add nutrients for these to get a full fermentation.

There are also commercial yeast varieties for specific alcohols, such as whiskey or rum, if you choose to try and make alcohol out of traditional materials like corn or molasses. But, until you understand, and become proficient at the process, I recommend sticking to the easier way, which I am covering here. You'll still be amazed by what you can produce!

Buy the cheapest white sugar available; bulk food stores are a good option, or watch for sales. Invert sugar or dextrose will ferment slightly faster and slightly cleaner, but can cost twice as much. You won't find that much advantage for distilling; although I do use those sugars for fine wines that I will be aging (these milder sugars don't compete with the subtle fruit flavours as much). In making moonshine however, you are just stripping the alcohol out of the liquid as fast as possible.

You may wish to calculate the amount of sugar needed to produce a particular percentage of alcohol, based on the limits of the yeast you are using. You will need approx 17g of sugar for every 1% x litre of alcohol you want to make. So, for example, if you want to make 23L of a 15% alcohol wash, you need 17 x 23 x 15 = 5865g or 5.865 kg of sugar.

So, when you buy yeast, ask what the maximum level of alcohol it may produce, and use that percentage (in the formula) to calculate how much sugar you will need. After all, no sense using more sugar than you need, only to leave it in the wash and end up pouring it down the drain.

And, while we're on the topic, don't try to re-use your wash after distilling. Even if you have a little residual sugar left, it isn't worth it. Dead yeast, boiled wash, bad colour...forget it. Start fresh each time. You'll find if you try to re-use your old wash, the new yeast won't like it, and may not ferment very well. It also won't taste nearly as good and you'll be wasting sugar and doing more end-filtering. The exception to this rule is for sour-mash whiskey, which I'll cover in a later chapter.

Let's assume you are using a yeast that will give the most return possible, the above-mentioned turbo yeast for example (which gives 20 percent). Using the above calculation, you would need 7.82kg of sugar. This is close enough that you can just round up to 8 kg of white sugar (Turbo yeasts recommend 8 kg for a 23 litre wash - but you can make any combination of volume that works for you).

Start by making sure your bucket/container is clean and sterile. Either use a chemical cleaner made for wine sterilization (Potassium metabisulfite for example) or boiling water will work fine too.

Assuming a batch of 23 litres, begin with about 15 litres of hot water (use distilled, good tasting tap water, or filter it using a Brita or similar filter. If your water has high chlorine content, or off flavours, this may translate into a bad taste in the wash. Chlorine can also inhibit the yeast from growing.

Add the sugar and stir well to fully dissolve it. (If you have water with high chlorine content, and you don't filter it, leaving the wash standing for a few hours before adding the yeast will allow much of the chlorine to evaporate off.) However, add the sugar to the water while hot.

Add yeast nutrient (if it isn't included with your yeast), and stir it in (follow directions on package for how much to use...it varies with brand, but don't add too much either). If adding separately, divide it in half and add half at beginning and the other half a few days later. Too much nutrient all at once can stress the yeast, since there are often ammonia compounds in it.

Add cold water to bring the volume to about 23 litres. (I put a mark on the outside of my bucket after carefully measuring out 23 litres)

When the temperature is below 90 degrees Fahrenheit (higher temperatures can kill yeast), add the yeast and stir well into the sugar water. Cover with a tightly woven cloth, secure with a string or elastic band, and set in a reasonably warm place (room temperature is fine).

Fermentation will begin within a day or two (depending on the yeast you've chosen). If you aren't familiar with the smell of fermentation, it will be much like the odour of bread baking...quite pleasant! You will notice bubbling and possibly a 'head' forming on top of the liquid, especially when you stir it. That is perfectly normal. Stir it vigorously once or twice a day for a minute or two. This gives the yeast some oxygen in the wash, and keeps the fermentation moving along. (You don't *need* to stir it, but it will ferment much more slowly if you don't).

Temperature will also affect the speed of the fermentation. Too cold and it will grind to a halt. Conversely, warmer temperatures will speed it up.

After a week or two, (even faster if you use one of the new, faster turbo yeasts), you will notice the fermentation has slowed to nearly a halt. Taste the wash (it won't hurt you…just sugar water remember?!). If it is still quite sweet but the fermentation has stopped, you may be dealing with a 'stuck ferment'. Add a bit more yeast nutrient or (even better) distiller's nutrient (maybe a teaspoon or so). Stir vigorously to circulate with the yeast and it should start up again. Be sure temperature isn't too cold.

If you want to save a little money on yeast, there is a technique that will stretch your dollar a bit. It does require you to have additional yeast nutrient however (and I recommend 'distillers nutrient' for this):

When your fermentation is good and active, say a few days in…(again, depending on the yeast), start a new wash with sugar in a different container, but leave it a gallon or so short in volume. Then take a gallon (4 litres) of the actively fermenting wash and add it to the new wash. You will also need to add a couple spoonfuls of nutrient to the new wash since there won't be much to feed the yeast. The actively fermenting yeast in the gallon you add will start the new batch fermenting. You can then add back a gallon of plain sugar water in the first, active wash.

Although you could in theory keep this going indefinitely, I think it is good to start with a new batch of yeast periodically. You may also not want to keep producing that quantity of hooch either! Note that this technique won't work as well if you wait until the *end* of the fermentation, since most of the yeast will have died off, and there won't be much live yeast to start the new batch with. Use an actively fermenting wash to add to the new batch.

When the wash is done fermenting, (1-2 weeks usually) you should notice that it no longer tastes sweet, and has a distinctly alcoholic flavour and smell! Once you get to this stage, stop stirring it. In a few more days, you will see the liquid clearing and a layer forming at the bottom of the bucket. That's exactly what you want. That layer, called the *'lees', or 'dregs'* is the dead yeast and other solids that have settled out. The clearer the wash, the cleaner the result will be, especially with freeze distillation. To speed up the process, you can use a clearing agent, called *'fining'* in wine terminology. This will produce clearing in a day or so, but isn't a necessary step. The wash will clear naturally in a few days if left undisturbed. If you want to spend a few extra dollars to speed it up, then go for it.

There are various brands and types of fining agents. Visit your local wine store for choices, or online. Some types include kieselsol, Sparkolloid, bentonite (a type of clay), chitosan, isinglass, gelatin, and even egg whites have been used. I would stick to bentonite since it is a more neutral agent. Sparkolloid is good too, but works more slowly. I would avoid egg whites since they could cause foaming in the tank, especially at the higher temperatures you will be working at, and some people may be sensitive to eggs. Chitosan and Kieselsol are often sold as a set, in sealed liquid envelopes as 'fining agent A' (negatively charged Kieselsol) which is added to the wine first, and then 'fining agent B' (positively charged chitosan) added a day afterwards. Beware though that Chitosan is made from shellfish exoskeletons, which also could be an allergy issue for some people. Please research, ask questions and know what you're adding to anything you intend to eventually consume! Bentonite is effective, and about as neutral as it gets, which is why I like it (I use it in winemaking!).

Another point to make is that if the fermentation is still active, this can cause foaming in the tank when heat distilling (more of a problem with pot distillation). So, either be sure the fermentation is over, or you can use a 'distilling conditioner' or 'foaming agent', which will prevent the problem.

At this stage, you can siphon off the cleared liquid into a still or containers for freeze distillation, and we're ready to begin!!

If you've never siphoned before, it's relatively simple. Use a hard plastic 'J' tube from wine store, which has a flexible plastic hose on one end (see photo). On the end of the hard tube will be a removable small plastic nipple (see the little red thing in the bucket), which prevents the lees from being sucked up into the still. You want the cleared wash only. The rest you can throw down the drain (won't hurt the plumbing or the environment…it's all natural remember?). To siphon, you need to have the bucket of wash raised above the level of the still or freezer containers, since siphoning relies on gravity. So, put it on a counter or chair high enough to keep siphon going. Then, I use a clamp to attach the rigid part of the tube in the liquid so it's just above the bottom of the lees. Don't put it right in the lees or you'll draw it into the tube. Make sure the flexible part of the hose reaches entirely into the still or container below or you'll be cleaning it off the floor!

(If you don't feel comfortable siphoning, or can't get the container high enough yourself (it will weigh quite a bit), you can very carefully use a pitcher or other food safe container to scoop out the wash and pour it into the still. Have it already in place on the stove or nearby, so you don't have to lift it either. Just be careful not to disturb the lees at the bottom of the bucket any more than possible.)

To start the siphon, suck hard on the flexible tube to draw the wash through and start it flowing. You'll be able to see it flowing through the tube. As it approaches the end, quickly put the hose into the still. Liquid will continue to flow naturally due to gravity. Towards the end, you can very carefully tip the bucket to get all of the wash, but take care not to draw the lees in. A little won't hurt, but better not to have any if possible.

Siphoning depends on gravity

30

If you aren't comfortable 'sucking' on the end of the hose, then do it this way…fill the hose and tube completely with water and put your fingers over the ends. Quickly put the rigid tube into the wash, and the other end into the still and let go of both ends simultaneously. This is a bit tricky to catch onto at first, and you won't be able to use the nipple on the end of the rigid tube, so you'll have to be careful about drawing in the lees. Sucking is easier, and it won't hurt if you get a little wash in your mouth. And, since the alcohol is boiled out of the wash, you won't be transferring any germs to the moonshine. The temperature is too high, and nothing could live in the high alcohol content of your distillate.

How you 'extract' or distil the alcohol depends on what you want to spend, and how comfortable you are with equipment.

There are basically two methods. One is heat distillation, the other freeze distillation.

Siphoning is the same for both, you would simply siphon into a still boiler for heat distilling, or separate containers for freezing.

A note on transferring your wash…as I said before, you can also transfer the wash into the still with a pitcher, bucket, pot, or any other food grade container. What you will find is that 23 litres of liquid will weigh quite a bit! If you're a strong guy, no problem. Most strong guys can lift that much weight, but some women may have trouble. A litre of water, not counting the sugar, weighs about a kilogram, or about 2.2 pounds. So, a 23-litre batch of wash will weigh about 23 kilograms, or about 50 pounds, plus the weight of your still! So, what you could do is have your still in position where your heat source is, then scoop the wash into it from your fermentation bin. Or if you're doing freeze distillation, scoop it into containers for the freezer.

OK, on to distillation methods!

Freeze Distillation

Freeze distillation requires almost no technical knowledge, or equipment other than some plastic jugs. (In truth, what you are actually doing is concentrating the alcohol, not distilling..also called fractional freezing). Heat distillation however, will produce a cleaner, higher alcohol content result. In freeze distillation, you need only freezer space large enough to freeze, or partly freeze the amount of wash you have made, along with plastic containers to put it in…and…use plastic, not glass, which may break.

So how does freeze distillation work? Well, alcohol doesn't freeze as readily as water, (ethanol freezes at -114 degrees Celsius or -173 degrees Fahrenheit, compared to water which freezes at 0 degrees Celsius or 32F), so the alcohol will remain liquid, while the water around it freezes. That's why a form of alcohol is used in windshield-washer fluid or antifreeze…it won't freeze up on your windshield. But I stress again, NEVER use windshield-washer antifreeze for drinking! It is NOT safe to drink!

When the water has mostly frozen, the liquid that is left will be partly alcohol. You simply pour it off, strain it or filter it off. I say partly alcohol, because it is not possible to get 100 percent pure alcohol no matter which method you use. Even with heat distillation, you will be doing well to get 75% to 80% alcohol on the first distillation (but that is still 150 to 160 proof!). You can achieve higher percentages by re-distilling the first distillation, but it's a lot of effort you don't need to go through.

Freeze distillation won't achieve as high an alcohol percentage as heat distillation, simply because it is harder to separate the water and alcohol using cold than it is using heat. I'll explain heat distillation shortly.

The equipment you will need for freeze distillation will depend on how you intend to freeze it. If you have the freezer space, you could use something like an expanding water jug. They are squarish, have a spout on one end and collapse when not in use...the type used on camping trips for taking drinking water. They will allow you to alter the shape to conform with the freezer space, but depending on the size, will take up a fair chunk of space...I've seen them up to 4 gallons in size. The spigot at the bottom will allow you to drain out the hooch after it freezes.

Caps glued together

Even easier is to use a few 2 litre soda jugs. Fill the containers *nearly* full and stand upright in a freezer with the caps a bit loose to allow for expansion. Freeze for several hours until it is mostly frozen. Using other tops, drill holes in them and firmly tape or glue them together. Attach an empty jug onto the frozen one. Turn the frozen one on top and let the ethanol drain into the empty one on the bottom. You can use a series of these, depending how much wash you make (if you made 23 litres as above, you will need at least 13 jugs...12 for freezing the wash and at least one for collecting it (you can empty it after each one drains). And, they won't take up as much space as a larger container. Again, be sure to _leave some air space at the top of the jug_ for expansion, & the cap a bit loose or you will end up with moonshine bombs in your freezer!

Alternately, if you don't feel like gluing together lids, you could just pour the unfrozen alcohol through a sieve and into a container or jug. I'd use a funnel a bit larger than the sieve, and don't pour too fast or it may overflow! It may take an hour or so for it to drain down.

Alcohol drains down, while ice remains at top

One thing to remember with freeze distillation is that you need to have a very clear wash to start with. Therefore, some form of clearing or fining agent after the wash has fermented out would be helpful...either that, or wait a week or two for it to clear naturally. Any cloudiness left in the wash will be present in the final result.

This also means that freeze distillation won't work quite as well with traditional spirits as it will with this basic formula wash just using sugar. More of the congeners or off flavours will transfer and be retained in your product. These off-alcohols are more easily removed with heat distillation.

If you want to take more time and allow your wash to clear naturally (and this can take a few days to a few weeks), it would be best to transfer the wash into a secondary fermentation vessel to avoid contamination and evaporation of the alcohol presently in the wash.

This will mean a glass (preferably) or plastic vessel (carboy) large enough to hold the volume of wash you made, a rubber bung, and a fermentation lock. A little water or sterilizer solution in the trap allows gases to escape, and no air to enter. You should be able to find these glass carboys for under $30 each, and a few dollars more for the bung and fermentation lock. As with everything else, they will last for years.

It may take a couple days in the freezer to freeze out the water, depending how much alcohol is present. The higher the alcohol content, the longer it will take to freeze, (also depending how cold your freezer is set - most are adjustable, so you can turn it right down for better results).

Because the process is less efficient than heat distillation, you may want to do the freezing process a couple times in order to effectively freeze out all the water and concentrate the alcohol in the subsequent freezing.

You should be able to achieve 25 to 30% ABV (alcohol by volume) on the first freeze, which may be adequate enough for your needs (50 to 60 proof). You will need to judge it for yourself.

If you are satisfied with the concentration of alcohol you get from the first freezing, great! If not, repeat the process one more time using what you separated off. The wash will freeze less this time, since the concentration of alcohol is much greater. So, it could take even longer in the freezer to solidify the water. You may also want to turn the freezer down lower if you can. The higher the concentration of ethanol in water, the longer and colder temperature it will need to freeze. But, the colder it is, the higher the strength of your alcohol will be.

Then, after you refreeze, drain it off again and you'll have a more concentrated alcohol. Heat distillation (with a still) will always be more effective at concentrating the alcohol content the first time. But, you can't beat the cost of freeze distillation…nearly free! And, if you have cold winters in your part of the world, just put the containers outside when the temperature is below freezing, the colder, the better!

Again, the key to this method is using as clear a wash as possible since more impurities will be in your final product than with heat distillation. For this reason, I don't recommend it for fermenting grains since you will be retaining all of the congeners or off-flavour alcohols produced, which you can more effectively separate out with heat distillation. It would also be advisable to charcoal filter the distillate to further improve the flavour.

Using sugar and yeast as in my technique above won't produce any significant amount of harmful substances. It's just sugar, water and yeast after all. You may read copious warnings on the internet about going blind from drinking moonshine. Indeed, this is possible using the wrong equipment or ingredients, but not with my method. If you can eat sugar and bread (which contains yeast), and drink water, this will be no more harmful as long as your equipment is also made of food safe materials.

If you follow the practice of old time moonshiners and use backwoods creek water (which could contain farm runoff, pollution, bugs, or bear poo), old metal containers for brewing and distilling, then yes, you could produce something that will harm you. Please use clean water and ingredients!

But freeze distillation, as simple as it seems, is the easiest way to get concentrated alcohol to start making your own drinks!

Another thing to bear in mind is, that besides a neutral spirit, it is also possible to make an easy 'liqueur' by this freezing method. For example, if you wanted to make some 'apple-jack', you can buy some reasonably priced apple juice, add some sugar and ferment it. Then, when complete, freeze concentrate this and you will have a liqueur style apple drink. You could even freeze a commercial wine to make a fine brandy-style drink.

The same can be repeated with any fruit juice you like. You can even add a little extra sugar when fermenting to make the end product a little sweeter, or sweeten it afterwards with some simple syrup (recipe for this later). Here is a sample recipe:

Freezer Apple Jack

Ingredients

10 - liters or quarts of apple juice or cider
2 - kilograms (4 1/2 pounds) of white sugar
1 - package Turbo yeast or high yield wine yeast
1 - teaspoon yeast nutrient
1 - package of wine fining (clearing) agent (optional)

Directions

- Mix sugar, apple juice, yeast and nutrient together
- Ferment until yeast dies, and a sediment layer forms at the bottom
- Rack or carefully pour off clear liquid from sediment
- If desired, use a wine fining (clearing) agent to further clear the wine
- Fill plastic jugs with wine, leaving a couple inches of expansion space
- Freeze for a couple days in a cold freezer
- Drain alcohol off of frozen juice
- If desired, refreeze and repeat. Bottle in glass.

From ten liters of juice, you can reasonably expect about 3 liters of apple jack at about 25 - 40 percent alcohol, depending on many factors, including the yeast you used and whether you repeated the freezing process.

Heat Distillation

Heat distillation is a more complex method, with some additional, more expensive equipment required (most notably, some form of still). There is also a bit more of a learning curve and more technical knowledge required, but it is faster and more efficient than the freeze method, giving a cleaner, purer result.

The method of making the wash is the same in both freeze and heat distillation, so follow the instructions above to make a wash. It is not quite as important to have a perfectly clear wash however...you can get away with a bit of cloudiness. Be sure that fermentation is done though. Do not distill an active fermentation. This could cause severe foaming in the still.

You could make a still yourself if you were adept at welding stainless steel or copper, but there are good commercial units available. I list some sources at the end in the appendix. They run from a small capacity tabletop unit that sells for about $200, to larger capacity one that sells for $400 or much more. Not cheap, but a good stainless steel or copper still will last for decades and you will most likely re-coup the cost in the first few months (depending how much you use it) in money saved by making it yourself.

Heat distillation works simply because alcohol boils at a lower temperature than water. Where water boils at 100 degrees Celsius (212 degrees Fahrenheit), alcohol (ethanol) boils at about 78.3°C (about 173 degrees Fahrenheit) at sea level under ideal atmospheric pressures. Therefore, the ethanol contained in the wash will begin boiling long before the water does.

Heat distillation simply involves heating the wash enough to evaporate the alcohol, but not the water. As with freeze distillation, you'll never achieve 100 percent separation, since there is always a bit of water that 'hitches a ride' with the alcohol! But since we're not dealing with solids, but entirely liquid, it is more efficient than freezing. That said, there are also more dangers involved since we're talking about higher temperatures, and a more dynamic process. So exercise safety and care with your equipment and procedures. I recommend purchasing a commercial unit, but if you choose to make a homemade still, be sure you know what you're doing!

There are basically two types of heat distillation for our purposes, pot distillation and reflux distillation.

Pot distillation uses a short column to collect the distillate, or none at all. This has advantages in that it preserves more of the flavours and aromas of the mash or wash. For instance, if you were making traditional rum from molasses and sugar cane, more of the complex esters…what gives rum its smell and taste…would be retained in the alcohol. The same is true for corn whiskey, gin, etc.

Pot distillation is how all of the early pioneers made alcohol, before science and the understanding of reflux methods. Pictures of early stills show a copper tube wound in coils coming out of a large copper pot. This method would still work today if you wanted to make traditional spirits. Much care, not to mention time, is required in preparation and fermentation, to ensure you get the flavours you want.

However, using the methods here, with plain sugar, there is no advantage to using a pot still. Many commercial distillation units have the ability to use a shorter or longer column, allowing you to change between pot and reflux.

With reflux distillation, a long column (around 3 feet or more) is used, which allows a purer distillate or evaporate to reach the top of the column. Fewer additional aromas or flavours will be present, which in this case, is what we want. With plain sugar, you're trying to obtain a nearly flavourless product.

In either case, as the vapour comes out the top of the still, it is necessary to 'reconvert' it into a liquid before it reaches your collection jug. Take my word for it, you really don't want alcohol vapours to come shooting out the end of your hose, especially if you have a gas stove. Think flash fire or instant explosion! (I also **_strongly_** recommend an electric stove or an induction cook top for that reason!). (Which ever still you choose, please test it using water first, to make sure there are no leaks or other problems.)

How a condenser works

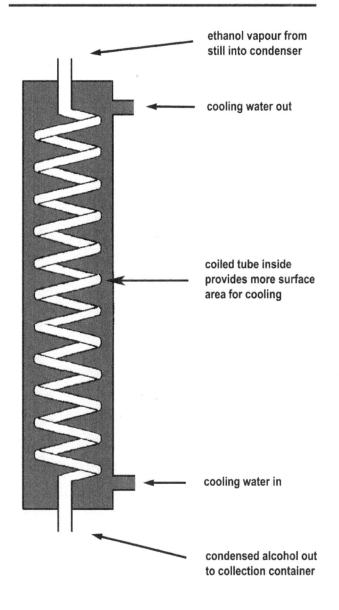

ethanol vapour from still into condenser

cooling water out

coiled tube inside provides more surface area for cooling

cooling water in

condensed alcohol out to collection container

So now, you need to have a way to cool this gaseous ethanol back into liquid ethanol. This is done by using cooling water at the top of the still, in a small unit called a condenser.

The condenser contains a coiled copper tube connected to the still at the top, and a flexible tube at the bottom. Around this coil is a housing through which cool water runs. This cool water circulates around the coil and the vapour entering the coil is 'condensed' back into a liquid, which then flows out of the bottom tube and into your collection container.
Voila… moonshine!

That's it in a nutshell. Now for a bit more detail.

I'm going to assume for now that you've purchased a commercial still from one of the sources available. This will be stainless steel, copper, or a combination thereof, with some plastic hoses.

Whatever the volume of the unit is, be sure NOT to fill it entirely. You have to leave some room for the liquid and vapours to expand at the top of the tank. Too much pressure could build up and send the wash shooting out the top of the unit! That would not be good.

So, leave a few inches of headspace when filling the tank.

Be sure to clean your still before using. Generally speaking, don't use soap for cleaning inside these units. It sometimes leaves a film, and can affect the taste and quality of the distillate. Use boiling water to sterilize the tank. To clean it more thoroughly, use a few links of stainless steel or copper chain (often sold with the units), and some water to basically 'scrape' it clean on the inside, shaking it around and dumping it out.

The column you use may or may not contain packing. You <u>should</u> use something, and there are two kinds of packing most commonly available. One is known as raschig or rachig rings, basically small ceramic rings. The other is copper packing, which essentially looks like long copper scrub pads. Both work fine, but preference is given to

Copper mesh for packing

the copper packing. It gives a purer tasting result, which requires no, or less carbon filtering. Distillation suppliers sell both, but you could also use <u>(solid) copper</u> pot scrubbers from a store (not with soap). In a pinch, you can even use clean small pea-sized gravel, but this would be a last choice.

Packing helps to maintain a constant heating rate in the column and provides a much bigger surface area than just the column walls themselves where the vapor can condense, but without interrupting its flow upwards and the flow of liquid downwards. Essentially, the packing provides more surface area where vapor can constantly condense into liquid then re-evaporate. This is called reflux, hence the type of still.

Whichever packing you choose, be sure to boil it first to remove any impurities, and don't ram it into the column like canon ammunition, just loosely fill the column. After all, you don't want to block the vapor, just help it evenly move up the column. Note that you will have to remove it and clean it regularly after use…maybe not every time, but every third time or so is fine. Boiling to clean raschig rings is fine. For the copper, a mild solution of lemon juice and salt will clean it up nicely, just soak it and you will see it brighten. Follow cleaning by a good rinsing, then boiling the copper. It doesn't take very long, and will help keep a good tasting product. Eventually it will need to be replaced, but it will last quite a while with care.

To set up your still, you will also need a method of tracking the temperature of the vapor in the tank. You can either use a thermometer at the top of the tank, or at the top of the column. I think the top of the column is best, since that will give a truer indication of when the boil has reached a critical level. One may come installed on your unit. If so, great! If not, see below.

If you use a thermometer on the tank itself, you can use a traditional thermometer in a rubber bung or grommet. If you opt for the top of the column, it is easier to use a probe attached to a digital readout thermometer (the kind used for oven roasting, available at hardware stores), for two reasons. First, it will be difficult to read a thermometer at the top of the column, and you may not have the ceiling height since the column will already sit very high on the stove. The exception would be if you use a freestanding hotplate instead of a stove. If this is the case, you should use it on a non-combustible surface, such as a concrete basement floor, patio stone, etc. It can take several hours to do a 'run', and the heat build-up could easily scorch a counter top or floor, or worse, cause a fire. Again,

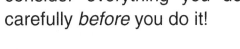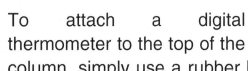

consider everything you do carefully *before* you do it!

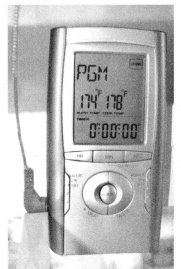

To attach a digital thermometer to the top of the column, simply use a rubber bung from a wine store of the appropriate size to fit *tightly* into the top. Drill a small diameter hole through the centre of the bung (smaller than the probe diameter) (freeze bung first to make drilling easier), and slide the probe end through the bung. Fit the bung tightly into the top of the column. The probe will have a wire attached to it that will plug into a digital readout (meat thermometer from a hardware or house wares store is fine). You can place this near the still where you can easily monitor the progress.

So, now you are ready to begin!

Siphon or pour the cleared wash into the still tank, allowing some air space at the top (don't fill it right up!). The column will attach using clamps and rubber gaskets. Don't forget the rubber gaskets.

They provide an airtight seal (you can also use cork provided they are

The column clamped firmly on the kettle   made to fit exactly). Tighten the clamp well and be sure the column is firmly attached.

You will need to attach the water hose to a water source, such as a kitchen faucet, for cooling the condenser. Attach it, and <u>be sure</u> it runs freely through the system. The water flow doesn't need to be terribly fast, just enough to cool the vapour. The water coming out of the condenser should be cool or only slightly warm. If it is hot, it may not cool the vapour sufficiently to turn it into a liquid. Again I stress, you don't want ethanol vapour escaping into the room.

Cooling hose/tap connection

Once you have it all set up on the stove or hotplate, turn it on fairly high. It will take some time to heat up, depending on the volume of your tank. A batch of 23 litres could take up to 30 minutes to reach critical temperature, during which time you won't need cooling water, but be sure to turn it on when the temperature nears the alcohol boiling point! A clue it is reaching the alcohol boiling point is that the still will become quieter. When it starts, similar to a kettle boiling, it will be noisy, metal is expanding, water is roiling in the boiler, but when it starts to boil, it quiets down...that's a clue you're nearly ready. You can also carefully feel the column. It will be hot near the bottom, so be careful not to burn yourself, but as the distillate rises up the column, it becomes hotter and hotter higher up. As it nears the top, it is getting ready to produce alcohol. Be there, and be ready!

It is common practice to collect the first few tablespoons of alcohol and discard it (or keep it for cleaning, etc.). The first ounces will contain any congeners, fusel oils and 'off flavour' alcohols such as methanol. Don't worry, there won't be enough to harm you, even if you don't set this first bit aside, but it may be present in trace amounts. It will just help your end result taste and smell better if you remove the first couple of ounces. These are called 'fore-shots'. Since methanol is produced from pectin and pulpier parts of fruit, you can limit the amount of methanol in ferment by using pectic enzyme when starting to ferment if you are using fruit. This is available from any wine supply store.

The last alcohols out of the still, the 'tails', will also have some off flavours, although not as bad as fore-shots. The middle part is where most of your best alcohol will be, and that is called the 'heart' or 'hearts'. Oh, and use glass or stainless steel to collect the alcohol. High alcohol distillate often can react with plastic, and that's never good!!

If you're using a digital thermometer with an alarm, you can set it to come on at a temperature just before the alcohol starts to run, say at about 170 degrees Fahrenheit (about 76 Celsius). This will alert you to make sure the cooling water is on, and to collect the 'fore-shots'. Be sure to have different containers handy in which to collect the fore-shots and ethanol. A 23 litre batch, fully fermented from 8 kg of sugar, should produce a little under an Imperial gallon, or a bit more than a US gallon at about 80% alcohol. Depending how efficiently your still operates, your results may vary from 70% ethanol (140 proof), to 85% (170 proof). If you have a professionally designed still, you may even do better. It is very difficult, even for the best commercial distilleries, to attain anything above 95%, so you should be happy with 75 to 80 percent from a first run. If you are really picky about purity, you can re-distil it to gain a higher percentage, but for the time it takes, it may be more trouble than it's worth. You would be doing well to get 90 percent even in a second run.

Whether you're using a reflux or pot still, be sure to have your outlet tube clear of obstructions or bends, so it can freely flow into your collection container. Also, do not allow it be under the surface of the distillate (moonshine). It should be above the alcohol and freely dripping or running into the container. If it gets below the level of the alcohol, it can build up backpressure and cause pressures to build up in the still itself. This could end badly. It's a simple enough thing to ensure, so do it!

Re-distilling can also help to improve the smoothness and flavour of the alcohol, since even more congeners are removed the second time around.

Even at 80 percent (160 proof), you will still have to cut it by half with distilled water to make it drinkable and comparable to commercial spirits on market (most whiskey, rum, etc. are 40% alcohol by volume or 80 proof).

The strength of your final spirit is your decision, but please don't try to drink straight shots of 160 proof/80 percent alcohol. This is very strong and could burn your mouth and throat. Nothing wrong with a few drops as a taste when it comes out of the still, to judge purity and strength, but even this little bit will demonstrate how strong it is! As a matter of fact, if you put a bit in a spoon and light it, it will burn!! (Ethanol will burn as low as 65% or 130 proof). That's why it's also important to keep it away from open flames, such as a gas stove. And...don't smoke around the still either!

If you intend to use a gas stove, be sure to have a long enough collection tube coming out of the still to be well away from the stove, just in case any vapours come out or you lose a bit of alcohol. It is very flammable and will catch fire immediately, especially with an open flame present. Also, keep the collection container below the level of the stove, since fumes, which are heavier than air, will fall to the floor.

The collection container should preferably be narrow-necked and a bit of cotton batting next to the outlet tube will prevent ethanol fumes from escaping and possibly igniting.

Common sense also says that distilling next to a gas furnace or water heater that may have a pilot light, or smoking, are also not good ideas.

In any case, it would be prudent to have a fire extinguisher handy, just in case! As the old saying goes, if you have it, you won't need it...if you don't have it, you will!!

With heat distillation (unlike freeze distillation), you will find that even if your wash is a bit cloudy, the moonshine coming out of the still will be perfectly clear, like water.

How long the run takes will depend on your heat source, type of still, and volume of wash. You should be able to do a 23 litre batch in about 4 - 5 hours. The key is to monitor the temperature throughout the run, and don't let it get too high. Higher temperatures may produce off flavours and smells by allowing other alcohols and by products to evaporate and contaminate your ethanol. Not that it would be harmful, just less pure. A cloudy distillate may also mean that you are running too fast and too hot. Slow and steady will produce the best result. Fast is NOT better! And, don't walk away from it for any length of time while it is distilling. Be in the room to keep an eye on it. The temperature will periodically go up a bit and the heat may need to be turned down slightly as it goes along. Keeping the temperature around 180 degrees Fahrenheit if possible (82 Celsius) will give the best result.

Depending on the model of still you purchase, it may come with a internal built-in electric element. Be sure to keep liquid above the level of the element, since you can ruin your expensive still if the liquid drops too low and you burn it out. Or even worse, if there are alcohol fumes in the still, it could cause an explosion.

Once the run is over, allow the still to cool down before trying to dismantle it or dump it. It will be very hot, and will take some time to cool before you can touch it. However, once you turn off the heat, you may also turn off the cooling water. Without a constant heat source, the distillation process stops almost immediately. When it's cool enough, you may safely dump the remainder down the drain. Again, it's all natural...sugar, yeast, etc. and won't cause any damage to the environment, septic or sewage systems.

Once you've finished collecting the distillate, clearly mark the container with what is in it, the alcohol percentage, whether or not it's been cut or filtered, etc. This way, next time you revisit it, you'll know exactly what it is and what needs to be done. Perhaps more importantly, some else who comes upon it will not think it's water or cleaning fluid or something else. And keep it out of reach of children or youngsters who shouldn't be drinking. Drinking straight moonshine could cause them serious injury.

Thoroughly clean and dry your equipment, and allow all of the water to drain out of your condenser...no sense letting it go stagnant between uses. Again, I would avoid using soaps or cleaners on the inside of the boiler. A long brush (available at wine stores for cleaning carboys) is helpful and letting it all dry thoroughly before storing it is a good idea. You don't want mold growing anywhere on or in it.

Some stills are sold with a piece of stainless steel or copper chain. Although noisy, you can put some water in the still, add the chain and agitate vigorously. This will dislodge anything on the inside of the still and help it stay clean.

A tarnished copper still can be cleaned with some lemon juice and a bit of salt. Rinse it around the inside, scrubbing with a long handle brush if possible. Follow by rinsing a couple times with hot water. The outside will also benefit by a good cleaning, and keep it looking new! You don't need to necessarily do this every time, but every 2 or 3 runs will keep it clean and in good shape.

Always finish by rinsing a couple times with clean water.

Using a Pot Still

The principle of using a pot still is the same as for using a reflux still, with one difference. The column on a pot still is much shorter, or non-existent, depending on the still design. You should always use a condenser though!

A pot still is used to preserve some of the flavours of the wash/mash you are fermenting, and would be used in making traditional spirits. The ingredients are mixed and fermented together (ground corn for example in corn whiskey, or molasses in rum). Following fermentation, the solids would be allowed to settle and the clear wash is siphoned off into either a secondary container (carboy) and allowed to clear further, or into your pot still. As I said before, it is best to get the wash as clear as possible.

Old time pot stills were often a copper body with a long coil of copper tubing (the 'worm') coming out of the top. Air was the method used to cool the evaporate back to a liquid alcohol because of the long coil length. However, it is still safer to use a cooling condenser. The stainless steel still I pictured has a two-piece column that can be used as a pot still by eliminating the lower section.

What I'll say about copper pots is that you must keep them clean. Copper will tarnish with time (like copper pennies), and if there is tarnish, this can be removed in the distillation process and end up in your alcohol. Also, copper can react with your mash if it's too acidic or alkaline. If you produce an off-colour distillate, DON'T drink it. Something in your mash has reacted with the copper, and the colour is a clue that it is no good. (Blue probably means ammonia is present). For that reason, I recommend a stainless steel still, and keeping your copper packing clean.

Be careful with fruit however. Contrary to popular belief, most fruit are alkalizing in nature. This can react with copper to produce off colour or flavour distillate. Not so much of an issue with stainless steel, but if you use copper packing, same advice. Proper pH for a mash or wash should be between 4.7 and 5.0, which is slightly acidic. This also helps keep the mash from growing bacteria. Buy some litmus paper or a pH testing kit.

You may have seen shows or internet sites that use a copper still with a 'thumper keg' between the still and the condenser. This thumper keg would collect any solids from the mash (many times the old timers would just ferment the mash right in the still, lumps and all). So, upon distillation, you get some of the corn or grain coming through the line. With the methods I outline, I don't recommend leaving solids in the still, since these will sit on the bottom and burn. Besides giving an awful flavour to your distillate, it may scorch the inside badly enough to ruin your still. Strain out the solids and clear it before adding the mash to the still and you won't need a thumper keg (also called a 'doubler').

Some people claim that the thumper keg 'doubles' the proof of the distillate. Poppycock I say. They add some of the mash to the thumper, or alcohol from a previous run, and claim that will double the proof. Well, if you're getting 150 proof from your still already, how can it double to 300? The highest it could ever go is 200 proof, which is pure alcohol!! As I said, even the best commercial distilleries can't achieve that. If you have an efficient still and do as I recommend in this book, you will achieve 150 to 160 proof without needing a thumper keg...no problem.

So, back to pot distillation...in order to make a traditional spirit and retain flavour, be sure to use enough of the main ingredient to provide that flavour. Lets take rum for instance. Traditionally, sugar cane syrup or sugar cane molasses is used. In this case, you can use molasses, which can be purchased in bulk. This would provide much of the sugar/sweetness to feed the yeast and produce alcohol. It is, in a way, like making wine in that the main ingredient will provide a flavour you're looking to retain. Unlike wine however, no aging is required before distillation. (If you are making a spirit in the traditional way, you may also want to acquire an oak barrel at some point in order to age the spirit after distilling. Be aware that that will cost you extra money and in most cases, your liquor will require aging from several months to several years!!). Aging a traditionally made spirit will definitely help smooth the flavour, but does take some time.

The pot distillation *process* is the same as reflux, with a couple of exceptions.

The column will be short or the unit will not have a column, in order to allow more of the congeners or flavours of the wash to evaporate through to the end. This is to retain more of the ingredient's flavours. You want rum to taste like rum or corn whiskey to taste like corn, etc. You should also be aware that carbon filtering isn't recommended, since you will lose a lot of flavour to that filtering. So, additional aging will likely be required to gain the best flavour.

Also, as with freeze distillation, a clearer wash will result in a better distillate, since there is less of a column to help 'purify' the wash evaporate. In other words, more can get through a shorter column, including solids and impurities. And, as I said previously, be sure your fermentation is complete, to prevent foaming, which would be even more of an issue with a pot still.

A pot still may also be used to ferment plain alcohol as previously discussed, but you will get a cleaner, less flavoured distillate with a reflux column.

Many commercial distilleries collect the 'heads' (first alcohol out of the still) in stages as it comes out, and similarly the 'tails' (last alcohol out of the still). These heads and tails contain many higher and lower alcohols that have flavour and smells that you may want to use to some degree. By collecting several different samples of these, you may choose to add a little bit of the heads or tails back into the 'hearts' (the middle, best and most productive part of the run), in order to adjust the balance of the alcohol.

A pot still will produce more of these heads and tails (also called feints). If you want to produce the best product possible, and this is more to do with a traditional recipe such as rum or whiskey, than with a sugar wash, then here is a procedure to follow.

As you distill, discard the first little bit for sure, since these will be unsuitable in any case. Then, use a series of small jars, say jam size or half pints, and as your run proceeds, fill and number each one sequentially. After it's over, put a coffee filter on each one. Let stand for a short time and let the space clear of any scents of your distillation. Then, come back and smell each jar, starting in the hearts and moving to the heads and tails.

You will notice that the heads smell much stronger and have more harshness to them. The tails will smell weak and less alcoholic. The hearts will have a pleasant, even sweet alcoholic smell.

The trick will be to figure out how much of the heads and tails you want to mix with the heads to produce your final product. Including more heads will make it stronger, but perhaps too strong. You want to smell the influence of the grain, corn or whatever, without having the congeners overpower the sweet hearts. More of the tails will serve to water down the quality and make it a bit more 'plain'.

Obviously this will take some practice to master, but it's a good exercise to do at least a couple times, especially when starting a new recipe. Once you've got your preferences nailed down, you won't need to do this every time, since your ingredients will be the same and your procedure should be the same.

You can reserve the remaining heads and tails and redistill them with the next batch or save them and do a run with these feints only. It won't be quite the same as the original recipe, but it will still produce decent alcohol.

In short, a pot still is more useful to retain part of the smells and flavour of your wash. You can also use it to distil a fruit wine for example, or by adding fruit to your wash (such as bananas) to make a fruit brandy. Soak the fruit in the wash while fermenting it, but be sure to filter or sieve them out before adding to pot still. The same goes for grains if you are making whiskey, etc. You don't want solids in your still. These will naturally fall to the bottom of the tank and will most likely burn. This can not only cause bad flavours in your alcohol, but may be very hard or impossible to get out of your still, possibly ruining it. A still is too expensive to take that chance!

Calculating Alcohol Volume

So how do you calculate how much alcohol you have produced? You can use a little tube called an alcoholmeter (makes sense doesn't it!).

This tube will float in your ethanol, and has a scale that you can read the level of alcohol you produced. The larger the alcoholmeter, the more accurate the scale, so get one at least 12 inches (30 cm) in length. If you find it too difficult to float this in a gallon jug, you can also buy narrow testing cylinders made for these meters.

It's important to know the percentage of alcohol (ABV: alcohol by volume) you produced, so you can calculate how to 'cut it'.

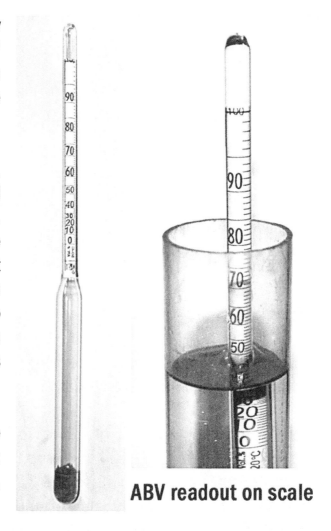

ABV readout on scale

Cutting is essentially adding distilled water to your moonshine to make it drinkable at an accepted level (generally 40%...or 80 proof). In some cases, such as making liqueurs, you may add it full strength when blending with other liquid ingredients, but you will still need to know what that strength is. Buying an alcoholmeter is not expensive, and as with the still, with care, will last many, many years. It is glass however, so a certain amount of care is needed to avoid breakage...ask me how I know...!

Cutting is simply a math calculation to achieve an end result. A simple example is: for 80% straight moonshine, adding an equal amount of water will give you 40% alcohol.

Let's say you wanted 2 litres of alcohol at 40% abv, but you had 70% distillate. How would you get the 2 litres at the right percentage?

The formula is as follows:

volume wanted x desired strength x $\dfrac{100}{\text{present strength}}$ = how much alc.
  (litres for eg.)   100   to use

So, in our example, the numbers would be:

2 litres   x $\dfrac{40(\%)}{100}$ x $\dfrac{100}{70(\%)}$ = how much alcohol
(end volume)   to use

2 (litres) x .4 x 1.43 = 1.144

Therefore, start with 1.144 litres of your 70 percent distillate and top it up to 2 litres with distilled water. You'll then have 2 litres of 40% hooch!

Now, before you have a fit trying to measure to such small amounts, a couple tablespoons here or there won't make any real difference! I guarantee that no one will be able to tell the difference between 40% and 41% strength, so even if you rounded your total up or down a bit, that's fine. Don't go crazy trying to measure to 3 decimal places!

Now you have your moonshine! What to do with it?!

If it is pure enough quality, you can cut it as above, drink it and enjoy it! It will be much like vodka, fairly flavourless.

However, if the flavour is still a bit harsh or strong, you can go through one more step of purification known as carbon filtering.

Carbon filtration

The use of activated carbon to filter liquids is commonplace. There are many water filters on the market available to filter chemicals, smells and tastes out of municipal tap or well water. The same principles apply to filtering ethanol.

It's important to note that if you are trying to make whiskey, rum, or other spirit straight out of the still, (besides moonshine or vodka), you won't want to carbon filter it, since this will remove many of the flavours you are trying to create in your liquor!

Basically liquid is run through these filters, which contain small particles of activated carbon. Activated carbon can be compared to tiny sponges full of holes, which trap impurities in pores on their surface, resulting in better tasting and smelling water, or in this case, moonshine!

It is important to use activated carbon meant for consumption. Do <u>not</u> use carbon meant for aquariums, since that is not as pure, and itself may contain impurities you don't want. There are also carbon filters meant for air and gas, which also aren't what you want. If you are going to the trouble of doing this, then please use the right product to get results you'll like!

Active carbon may also be made from a variety of sources, including coconut shells, peat, wood and stone. Most suppliers of distilling equipment and supplies will sell appropriate types and qualities of carbon. The best type to use for your purposes is a <u>stone based</u> carbon, sized 0.4 to 1.4 mm in size (.4 to .85 mm is even better). This is the best quality, and is also reusable. I'll explain how later.

If you want to filter your moonshine with the least inconvenience, you can go to a store and buy a water pitcher with a Brita filter, or from any other water filtration manufacturer. Use this to filter your 40 – 50 % alcohol. The advantage is convenience. The disadvantage is cost. These types of filters <u>will contaminate quickly</u>, and to my knowledge...are not re-usable. Not the best option in my opinion. They provide minimal filtration at a high price.

Carbon filtration setup

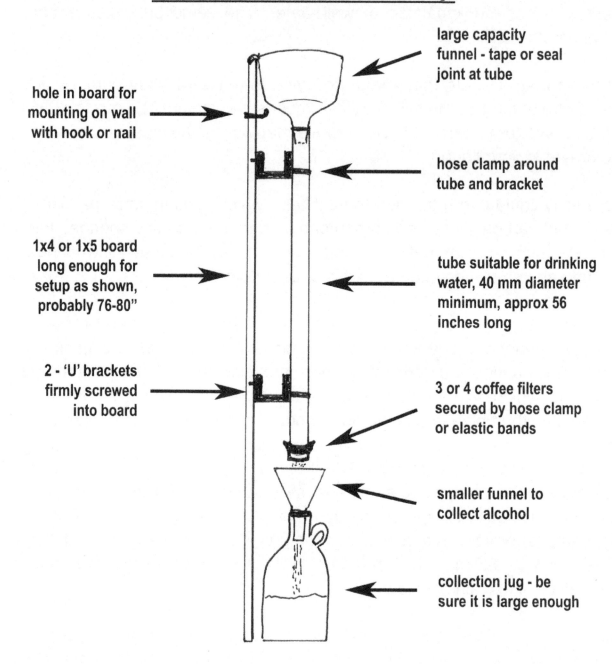

large capacity funnel - tape or seal joint at tube

hole in board for mounting on wall with hook or nail

hose clamp around tube and bracket

1x4 or 1x5 board long enough for setup as shown, probably 76-80"

tube suitable for drinking water, 40 mm diameter minimum, approx 56 inches long

2 - 'U' brackets firmly screwed into board

3 or 4 coffee filters secured by hose clamp or elastic bands

smaller funnel to collect alcohol

collection jug - be sure it is large enough

To manually filter a batch of moonshine, you'll need about 1.5 to 1.7 litres of carbon (it will come packaged in about this quantity, depending on manufacturer). See the appendix for sources of suppliers.

There are commercial filter units available, but here is how to make one for yourself. You will need a solid plastic water tube about one and a half meters (4 1/2 to 5 feet) long and about 40 mm (about 1.6 inches) wide (available at hardware or plumbing supply stores). Be sure to buy one acceptable for water supplies…again, we're drinking this stuff remember! You will also need a large funnel, two large metal U shaped brackets, two hose clamps a bit larger than the tube, a 1x4 board about 6 feet long, several coffee filters, a few strong elastic bands and some tape to seal the funnel to the tube. See the sketch for construction details.

To build it, secure the U-brackets (facing up) to the board with screws, and use the hose clamps to secure the tube to these brackets. Securely tape the large funnel to the top of the tube. You don't want it leaking all over the place! Use 3 or 4 coffee filters at the bottom of the tube (depending on their thickness) with several elastic bands or a hose clamp to hold them in place. You need several layers since there will be a bit of pressure on them due to the weight of the carbon and liquid (if you only use 1 or 2, they may break). Once you've built the filter, you can hook it to a wall with a securely fastened hook or nail. Be sure to make use a board long enough to allow room at the bottom of the filter for a collection container (large jug or jar).

In preparation of filtration, have the following ready:

- moonshine cut to no more than 50% alcohol in strength (100 proof). It can
  be filtered at higher proofs, but it is less effective and won't filter quite
  as well. So, dilute the ethanol with distilled water *before* you filter.
- And 4 litres of very warm filtered or distilled water.

Prepare the carbon as follows:

- Put the carbon in a large saucepan and add at least twice as much boiling water.
- Stir and let the carbon settle (it's a bit like stirring sand!).
- Pour the water off carefully and repeat 2 to 3 times until carbon is well saturated. This cleans it of any impurities and prepares it for the alcohol. (You may note a little black powder coming off the carbon. That's normal and is OK...best to get rid of it. The coffee filters also help to eliminate this powder should some remain during filtration).
- The last time, carefully and steadily pour the water and carbon into the tube. Try not to create any pockets of air...this would slow down filtration and make it less efficient. Give it a couple light taps just to eliminate air pockets

This process can get a bit messy, so it's better to do it somewhere where a bit of water on the floor won't matter...outside in good weather, basement, bathtub, deck, etc.

Once the carbon is in the tube, start by pouring the 2 litres of warm water in the funnel and let it filter through. Just as the water gets to the bottom of the funnel, pour in the alcohol. <u>Don't mix them</u>, but you want the alcohol to go in *right after* the water, so little or no airspace is created between the two liquids. The reason to use hot water is...it's easy to tell when the hot water finishes filtering through by temperature on the tube. You can feel the difference in temperature on the outside of the tube, so you know when the hot water is getting close to the bottom. Feel the tube as the hot water goes down...the alcohol will be cooler to the touch and you will be able to tell about when the alcohol is about to reach the bottom.

Now this may seem obvious, but...don't let the alcohol mix with the hot water. When you feel the warm water nearing the end of the tube bottom, remove the water container and have another empty container at hand to collect the alcohol. As the alcohol filtration nears an end, have another 2 litres of warm water on hand.

In the same manner as before, pour the warm water in the funnel just as the alcohol finishes going through. This will force any remaining alcohol in the tube to go through. Again, you will be able to tell by temperature when it nears an end...the alcohol will be cool, the newly added hot water will feel warm to the touch on the outside of the tube. A little bit of water with the alcohol won't hurt, but it would be a shame to lose any alcohol!

Again, remove the alcohol container once it has all filtered through, and have another container on hand to collect the remaining hot water, which you can throw out.

You will then have a very pure, clean tasting moonshine! Ready to drink, or make into whatever spirits you desire!

The beauty of using a good quality stone based carbon is that it is reusable many times. After filtration is complete, you can 're-charge' the carbon as follows using an <u>ELECTRIC</u> stove or oven...NOT GAS!

Boil the carbon in at least twice as much water for at least 10 minutes to boil off any trapped alcohols and impurities. You will smell them as they evaporate. These vapours can be volatile, so that's why I don't recommend using a gas stove! Keep your stove hood fan on to remove vapours from the room. Boil until smell subsides. Drain the water and throw it away. Then, have a large oven cookie sheet or shallow pan available. Drain the carbon and spread out on sheet. Bake the carbon at a temperature of at least 140 to 150 degrees Celsius or 300 Fahrenheit in an ELECTRIC oven for at least 2 hours. Please note, do not do this in a gas oven. The vapours may ignite and explode in a gas oven, and that could be disastrous. If you only have a gas oven, then stick to boiling the impurities off on the stove with the stove hood fan running. You may also want to crack the stove door open a bit to allow the vapours/smell to escape. Once you have done with the baking, the carbon is ready for use again. Simply repeat the process above. If you don't have an electric stove, perhaps you can beg the use of a friend or family members, just to purify your carbon.

I know this process may seem daunting at first and you may be wondering if you will be up to the task of doing this. Once you get the hang of it, the steps will soon become like second nature, and won't be so intimidating.

An alternative to building this unit is to use a small wine filter available from many suppliers called the Buon Vino. Although made for wine, a supplier in Canada sells carbon filters that fit the smaller unit (mini-jet). I don't believe these are re-usable as the loose carbon is, since the carbon is embedded into pads. Three of these are used at once then discarded after a batch is filtered. How much use you get out of these pads will depend on your distillate. Certainly freezer distillate would require more filtration than that from a commercial heat unit, but you should get at least a couple gallons filtered with a set of pads.

To use these, you soak the pads briefly in clean water and stack them into the filter (it will come with directions on how to assemble). Then run the filter for a couple minutes using clean water...at least 5 or 6 gallons. This is to get rid of any stray carbon bits that may come off pads. Then filter the alcohol. Again, cut the alcohol to 40-50 percent before filtering. This filtration will take much of the harshness out of the shine, and leave you with a very pleasing looking and tasting product.

Another alternative instead of building the column filter, although a bit less effective, is passive carbon filtering. Simply prepare the carbon as above and instead of adding to the column, add it directly into the distilled moonshine. Stir it every day for about 7 days, then strain it through a couple coffee filters into a glass container. Let it sit for a couple more days just to ensure that it is totally clear and the carbon has been filtered out. Although it's unlikely to hurt you in any way, seeing grey or black cloudiness in your alcohol just won't look very good. If any settles to the bottom, simply siphon off the clear alcohol into another bottle. This is a bit slower, in that it takes more time to do, but it's less work than building a filter.

Now, you will have several litres of 80 to 100 proof ethanol, ready to put to use! This moonshine will be relatively tasteless and odourless (much like vodka, so if you like vodka, you're all set!).

Do a rough calculation of the cost of ingredients for what you produced, and I'm sure you will be pleasantly surprised how economical it is! For example, if you can get sugar for say…$3 for 2 kilograms, Turbo yeast for about $5, that's only $17 for a 23 litre batch, plus the water and electricity. Even if we said $20, that's still pretty cheap to get 5-6 litres of moonshine! As I said previously, it won't take long to see the payoff for the initial cost of equipment.

In the recipe section, you will learn about various liquors and liqueurs and how to add flavourings and make this 'vodka' into a wide variety of drinks.

Filtering and Clearing

For many of the recipes you will read here, especially traditional ones for liqueurs, you will be adding many ingredients which will serve to 'cloud' or 'muddy' the appearance of your liquor.

In some cases, such as cream liqueurs or crème liqueurs, this cloudiness is natural and desirable to the appearance of the drink.

In other cases, you may want a clearer looking spirit to improve the appearance and get rid of microscopic particles of the ingredients.

There are a couple methods for doing this. The first is to naturally let the liquor sit upright for several days or weeks until it naturally clears. The suspended particles, because they are heavier than the alcohol and water, will eventually settle out and form a layer at the bottom of your container. Then, you simply siphon off the cleared liquor and bottle it, or pour it very carefully to avoid disturbing the sediment. Also see fining, from page 29.

The other alternative is to use a commercial wine filter, which you can buy or order at most wine supply or brew-it stores. There are simple and inexpensive ones that you simply pour through a filter, or more expensive ones such as Buon Vino, which use an electric pump to force the liquid through a series of filters to trap the suspended particles.

These are different from carbon filtering in that they won't remove the flavour from the liquor, or not much at least, compared to carbon filtering.

In the recipes, I try to keep it simple, and simply say that you can use coffee filters or allow the liquid to settle. That will work, but commercial filters *are* available if you wanted something fast and effective. Note, that this advice is mostly to improve the appearance of the liquor, not the taste!

Examples of commercial wine filters. Just do an internet search to see what's available in your area, or visit a local wine or brew shop to see if they carry or could order any.

Aging Spirits

Many people hold onto bottles of wine and spirits for years, thinking they will get stronger with age. That's largely folklore and old wive's tales. Many times I've heard something like..."That bottle of dandelion wine I found in Uncle Joe's garage sure was potent after sitting there for 30 years". In most cases, that just doesn't happen. It isn't possible for wine or spirits to GAIN in potency or alcohol just sitting around. The exception would be if it continued fermenting in the bottle. Most of the time, this would have resulted in 'bottle bombs' since the added pressure of gas release inside the bottle would have caused it to explode! And, in most cases, unless wine is stored properly, or had enough alcohol to preserve itself to begin with, it probably wouldn't even be drinkable after so long.

Aging of wines and spirits is largely done in bulk after production, in oak barrels that 'breathe'. This helps mellow them, lets trapped gasses escape, and imparts a certain character and colour, partly from the wood itself.

Although many wines will mellow in bottle with age if stored properly, both wine and spirits are better aged in bulk before bottling. Once bottled, spirits are sealed in a glass bottle with a screw top or sealed plastic cork. The aging process then largely ceases and any change will be to a lesser degree than wine for instance that may have natural cork sealers, which allow the wine to breathe. With commercially purchased spirits, the manufacturer has already aged them to where they taste best, so little is to be gained by leaving the bottle on your shelf for an extra 10 years!

So, if you decide to age your homemade spirits, invest in an oak barrel or two, as large as you think you can keep filled, and age it for a few months or years. Barrels are available in small sizes from about a gallon and up, although like I said, aging seems to work better in larger quantities. You will need a cool area where it can sit undisturbed for some period of time, and will have to be checked every once in a while. Wood breathes, and you will notice a small amount of evaporation over months of storage. This is called the 'angel's share'!

Oak barrels are available in (most commonly) American or French oak, and are available as untoasted, lightly, medium or heavily toasted. Toasting is essentially burning or charring the inside of the barrel. This imparts a smoky taste and aroma to the alcohol. The heavier the toasting, the smokier the flavour. This is especially apparent in scotches and whiskeys. Charring also helps remove sulphur compounds from alcohol and 'mellows' an immature liquor. The wood itself also imparts its own character. There is no substitute for aging in barrels for a few years, but you will need patience!

It's important to check the aging progress at least every month or two, since the flavour will deepen the longer it is in the wood. If you don't check it, at a certain point, you may find the flavour has grown too strong, especially if you have used a heavily toasted barrel. Also, the smaller the barrel, the faster the aging process, since there is a higher surface area to alcohol ratio than with a large barrel.

There is no need to cut the spirit to 40% in order to age it. A good strength for aging in oak is 50% alcohol. This way, if your spirit gets 'over-oaked', you still have the ability to cut it down with plain spirits. Had you already cut it, you would have few options if you found it overpowering other than blending with unoaked spirit, which is still perfectly OK.

Be sure to buy a barrel specifically made for alcohol. Don't go to the garden store and buy a barrel for putting flowers in, or a decorator barrel. They won't work and you'll be disappointed in the results, if they hold liquid at all!

If you are planning to use a barrel, be sure to prepare it. Sterilize it and fill it with plain water first. The wood needs to swell and expand. Better to do this with water, than your alcohol. Then drain it and fill it with your alcohol!

Short of buying a barrel, other slight shortcuts or 'cheats' to help soften your spirit is to add a bit of glycerine to it. A <u>few drops</u> will take the edge off. Glycerine is available at many wine stores and pharmacies. It is a perfectly natural product and won't cause any harm. Just don't overdo it! You can also buy oak chips, which you can soak the spirit in to give it added flavour.

A bit of clear honey can also be used to help take the edge off. And yet another choice is to use a little clear glucose (simple) syrup. A little sweetness, even if it's not much, can help to remove the sensation of bitterness, and give the impression of having been aged, even if it hasn't! YOU have to decide what the appropriate level is. Some people like their spirits sweeter, some don't. Same as coffee, some like it black, some like double-double!

Some commercially available spirits are now claiming 'maple-aged'. A shortcut to producing your own 'maple-aged' is to add a few spoons of pure maple syrup to your alcohol. And, the darker the maple syrup, generally the more intense the flavour and aroma. It will also help 'smooth out' the mouth feel also, making it seem more aged than it actually is.

Another shortcut to 'barrel age' your spirits is to take a piece of partly burned oak or maple (fireplace or fire pit) or another hardwood, and break it up into pieces (brush any loose ash off). (This is a technique in Tennessee whiskey, which uses sugar maple charcoal...then aged in American oak barrels). It won't take much, maybe 1/4 cup per litre. Clean it well and add the charcoal to your spirits for several days, shaking daily. Check after the first couple days or so until the desired flavour is achieved. If you accidentally 'over oak it', add a little more alcohol to thin down the flavour. Filter out the charcoal and let clear. Then bottle. Presto…aged moonshine! By the way, don't use pine or evergreen wood for this, since they contain saps and resins, that won't enhance your alcohol.

So now, if you've followed all the steps I've outlined above, you have a great basis to make your own moonshine cheaply, and even more important, safely! Remember, sterilize everything that will touch any part of your equipment and ingredients. Use clean, fresh, preferably filtered water and don't use sub-standard ingredients, or equipment that isn't stainless steel, copper or food grade plastic.

Read and re-read the instructions before attempting your first batch so you are comfortable with the process. It is easy and safe if you follow the correct steps.

Recipes and Creating drinks!

Now that you have made your first batch of moonshine, you may want to take the next step and make it into a variety of liquors and liqueurs. I include a variety of recipes here, meant to replicate some of your favorites!

The easiest way to do this is by using commercially available flavourings. There are different manufacturers of these, but one company I would recommend is Prestige. They have a wide choice of essence flavourings from absinthe to whiskey. You simply add these highly concentrated flavourings (generally a 20 ml bottle to make 750 ml of spirit) to your moonshine according to the directions, and you're off to the races for quick and easy liquors. I've used many of these and have been quite pleased. The company is based in Sweden, but are distributed worldwide. See the appendix for some sources of these flavourings.

Another flavouring source may be right in your own supermarket or liquor store. Most of these stores sell drink mix flavourings that you can use along with your moonshine to produce your own liqueurs. I've used these successfully for everything from crème de menthe to peach schnapps. You'll have to play around with whatever flavourings are available in your area, but I'll give some rough estimates in recipes below.

Another source of flavourings is a company called Soda Stream (formerly Soda Club). They make a wide range of natural and artificial flavour syrups, which you can mail order if a store is not near you. They are meant to be used to make your own carbonated soda or pop at home (using a carbonator you can also buy). However, I've used many of these to make liqueurs, even rather different flavours such as root beer schnapps. They even have sugar free flavourings for the calorie conscious!

The flavourings are quite concentrated, and will provide a very flavourful liqueur. As a rough guideline; use 40% (80 proof) alcohol half and half with the flavour syrup. This will give you a 20% abv (alcohol by volume) liqueur that you can then serve on the rocks or as a spritzer. A spritzer is simply some kind of wine or liqueur served with sparkling water or club soda.

For example, let's say you would like a lemon-lime spritzer. Mix the flavour syrup half and half with alcohol to give you the liqueur. Then mix this half and half with sparkling water or club soda. Serve on ice for a refreshing drink that has 10 percent alcohol, about what a glass of wine gives you. If this is too strong, you can add more soda or some of ice, which itself will help dilute it.

If the half and half concentration of syrup to alcohol is still too intense for you, try adding some distilled water to dilute the syrup. For example, 1/3 syrup concentrate, 1/6 distilled water and 1/2 alcohol, which would still give you about a 20% liqueur (using 40% alcohol), but slightly less intense flavour. Or, 1/3, 1/3 and 1/3 of each. You will soon find the right combination for your taste. I would recommend trying a small amount of each to get the balance right, then mixing a bottleful. You could even have a 'mixing' party, with your friends giving you some advice, or even mixing their own! Make it a fun social event, but don't go selling it to them!

I have a lot of fun walking through the supermarkets and specialty stores finding various flavourings, extracts and concentrates. Many are available, ranging from fruits such as cherry, apple, raspberry and blackberry. Remember Ribena syrup? It's basically concentrated black currant juice, but it makes an excellent liqueur mixed with some moonshine!

Peach syrup is also an excellent choice, and you'll find there are lots of other choices including crème-de-menthe, grenadine, margarita, etc.

Whatever your preference, make it to your taste…this is just a guideline!

Another tip is to wander through your local liquor store, making note of how much alcohol is in your favorite liqueurs or brandies. Then you'll have a rough idea how much you should have after mixing. There is no right or wrong, but if you're trying to imitate a commercially available drink, you want to come close. You'll find however that most traditional spirits such as gin, whisky, rum and vodka are about 40 percent alcohol (80 proof). Liqueurs tend to vary a bit more, but are usually lower, from 17 to 30%.

Making Traditional spirits

There are many and varied kinds of spirits on the market. One stroll through your local liquor store will tell you that. Many are of the same family...that is, whiskeys, rums, brandies, etc.

On the following pages, I include a wide range of spirits both produced the traditional way, those being from grains, grapes, etc., as well as those produced from plain liquor. Those being liqueurs, which use a base liquor and then are re-worked using fruit and other flavourings to produce a particular type of drink, such as Limoncello, Amaretto or Aquavit.

Distilled liquors are drinks produced from particular ingredients, fermented, distilled, aged then bottled. No further enhancement is usually done after the liquor is produced.

I will start with those first, followed by liqueurs, which use that spirit and either steep with fruits or spices to further enhance or gain a desired flavour and aroma.

One further note on making traditional spirits; it would be prudent to buy some litmus test papers (pH papers) to measure how acid or alkaline the wash is, as I covered earlier. (These are available at most chemists or pharmacies). Although this likely won't be a problem with a sugar wash, other ingredients such as fruit or molasses can produce an alkaline wash, which can react with copper, producing unwanted substances. Ideally, a wash should be between 4.7 and 5.0.

Your distillate should be clear. If it is another colour, don't drink it!! You've produced something besides alcohol, and it could harm you. It should smell and taste like alcohol. Re-check your equipment and ingredients! However, having followed my directions, this is very unlikely to happen.

Brandy

Similar to schnapps, a true brandy is a liquor distilled from fruit, most often grapes. If you have access to large quantities of grapes, press or juice them, and using a high alcohol tolerant yeast, ferment it to dryness. (As with schnapps, you can also ferment on the grape pulp itself for added flavour). Allow it to clear from the lees and run it through a pot still. If you don't have access to grapes, you can cheat a bit by using raisins, perhaps along with a handful of currants or dates to add a little flavour complexity. There are many regional types of brandy, Cognac for example, made in France.

Brandies are also aged for long periods of time, usually in large oak barrels, to enhance and smooth their character. But again, your wait can be lessened by using oak chips, glycerine or a little simple syrup to soften the flavour and shorten the time until you can drink it. Aging is always best, but not always practical if you don't have barrels or enough alcohol to barrel.

A basic starting recipe for 23 litres of must is:

> 10 kilograms of grapes or raisins, or a combination of both
>   (for more complexity, add a cup of chopped dates or currants)
> 3 tablespoons of acid blend powder or lemon juice
> 2 tablespoons yeast nutrient
> high alcohol tolerant yeast
> add water to make volume to 23 litres.

Juice and crush grapes, and chop or grind the raisins finely. In a fermentation bucket, pour on boiling water and add lemon juice and yeast nutrient. When room temperature, or at least below 90 degrees, add yeast. Cover fermentation bucket with a tightly woven cloth and secure with string or elastic. Stir vigorously at least once daily. After 6 or 7 days, strain out the solids with a plastic or stainless steel strainer or sieve, or with cheesecloth or straining bag. Squeeze well to get all of the juices out!

At this point, you are basically making a wine, and should use a secondary fermentation container (normally a glass carboy) of sufficient size to hold the must. You must fit a bung and an airlock to the top (available at wine store) to ensure an anaerobic environment. (Maintain water in the trap of the airlock). You can also continue fermenting on the fruit if you wish.

It is not necessary to stir the must in the carboy. You will know the fermentation is done when the wine begins to clear and a layer of lees forms on the bottom (it will be thick if you include fruit). Bubbles in the fermentation lock should have stopped also. All of this will take longer to do than a basic wash (could take several weeks), but should have a very nice flavour and aroma. Again, as I've been stressing all along, please make sure you sterilize everything that comes into contact with the must.

When fermentation has stopped and the wash has cleared, pot distil it.

If you're satisfied with the taste, great! To go one more step to finish it, you can use some toasted oak chips to achieve a more authentic flavour. Try about 5 grams of chips per litre of 50% alcohol. This will allow a bit of room to further dilute should the oak flavour be a bit too strong. One to two weeks on the oak chips is lots, then strain them out. Adding caramel will also help soften and give an aged look. About 15 ml per litre to start, but do it to your personal taste and appearance. Further aging for a couple months or more will also help smooth it out.

You can make a brandy style alcohol from other fruits as well. A general rule of thumb is to use 4 to 5 pounds of fruit per gallon of water, which is a bit higher than you would use for wine. However, to retain flavours and bouquet of the fruit through the distillation process, a bit more fruit is required. It is also helpful to ferment the fruit at a cooler temperature than you might for a basic sugar wash, also to retain more of the fruit essence. For fruits low in sugar content (some berries for example), you can add some sugar to produce a decent amount of alcohol.

The use of a hydrometer (similar to an alcoholmeter) will give you the 'specific gravity' of the must. To produce any appreciable amount of alcohol, it should be above 1.080 on the scale. The higher the specific gravity, the more sugar content is in the must and the higher the alcohol level will be. These are inexpensive and available at any wine store.

If you are using a fruit that is lower in sugar, you may need to add a bit to create enough sugar content to produce a decent amount of alcohol. You can also re-distill to add to the alcohol percentage.

Let's say your first run through the still only gives you 20 percent alcohol, but you want 40 percent. Use this distillate and re-run it through the still again. This will increase the alcohol level the second time through.

More work, but you won't have to buy a lot of extra sugar.

Calvados

Calvados is a type of brandy, originating in Normandy France, made from apples. Essentially it starts with an apple wine (or cider), which is then pot distilled to produce an eau de vie. Then, as with other brandies, aged for several years in oak barrels to give it smoothness and complexity.

Ingredients are fairly simple…apples and yeast! The art comes in choosing your apple varieties! Here, there are a multitude of possibilities. You'll want sweet apples to be able to generate a fairly good alcohol content to the wine, but you also want a little acid, as well as good aroma. Without a decent, strong fragrance, you might as well stick to fermenting sugar!

So, my recommendation would be to blend varieties of apples with these characteristics. What you use will depend on what is available to you! Sweet apples include Cortland, Delicious, Gala, Honeycrisp and Baldwin. Acidic apples are Northern or Red Spy (one of my favorites), Winesap, Greening and Pippin. Aromatic apples include MacIntosh, Russet (also a great apple), Empire and Fuji.

I would use approximately 50% sweet, 30% acidic and 20% aromatic to provide a good balance of flavour and bouquet.

The hard part of this liquor will be dealing with all the apples. If you take a totally purist approach on this, you will need about 10 kilograms of apples (just over 20 pounds) to produce a litre of Calvados. It will also be time consuming and difficult to cut up and juice all those apples. If you have access to a cider press, great…get to work! If not, you'll have to cut them up by hand, or use a food processor. You can core them if you want…not totally necessary. Don't peel them however; the peelings contribute a lot of flavour and aroma to the apples. So, decide how much calvados you would like, and scale your production accordingly.

If you wish, you can cheat a bit by adding a little water and even a bit of sugar to this, without adulterating it too much. You can then reduce the amount of apples you need slightly.

Method 1 - If you use a cider press, press the first time, then take the pressings and add about 20% of their volume in water. Mash together well and let stand for a bit, and then re-press. This will encourage a bit more of the sweetness out of the pulp...kind of an osmosis process.

Method 2 - If you use a food processor, add 10 to 15 percent of the volume in water and mix well (include the pulp). In this circumstance, also include the pulp in the fermentation. I like this method, simply because as I said earlier, the skins add a lot to the flavour and aroma of the final product. If you wish, add a little sugar to the must.

In either case, use a good quality wine yeast. No need for a turbo yeast here, since the most you will get will likely be 6 to 8 percent alcohol in your wine. Many purists insist that you should rely on wild yeasts, but as you have learned about me by now, I think that is horse and buggy thinking, and relies too much on crossed fingers and prayer. Better to use a known, reliable yeast (any yeast for fruit wines will do). A couple spoonfuls of yeast nutrient may also be necessary in the beginning, to get it going.

Ferment to dryness (taste it...should no longer be 'sweet cider', bubbling will have stopped...may even be bitter). Strain out the pulp (use a plastic or stainless steel strainer) & press to get as much juice and wine as possible.

If you have an alcoholmeter, see what level of alcohol you have. Hopefully at least 5%! Distil the strained wash with a pot still. Purists will say to distill it twice...use your judgement on that one. If you are happy with the concentration & flavour of the first run, then leave it at that. If not, re-distil.

This will definitely improve with age, especially aging in oak. If not, at least age it in bulk in a glass carboy for a few months.

To improve on flavour and age more quickly, add a few spoonfuls of simple syrup and a few drops of glycerine.

Bottle it when you are satisfied with flavour and smoothness.

Gin

This is a tough one to master at home. Although the primary flavouring ingredient in gin is juniper berries (specifically the immature green berry of *Juniperus communis*), there may be upwards of 30 herbs and botanicals found in commercial gin, the recipes are closely guarded secrets by the manufacturers. Some other ingredients may include coriander, cardamom, anise, orris root, cassis bark, ginger, lemon, grapefruit or orange peel, elderberry, caraway, liquorice, bitter almonds, cinnamon, angelica root or seeds, and nutmeg.

However, if you want to play around, I'd start with a good gin essence according to the style you like, mix it according to directions, then add 2 or 3 of the above ingredients, (depending what you like...I for one dislike nutmeg so I wouldn't personally use it), in small amounts, and age it all together for a few days, tasting each day to get an idea of strength. When satisfied, filter it through coffee filters into a clean bottle and enjoy! With a bit of experimentation, you'll find a combination you may like better than store brands!

For the more ambitious, here's a starting recipe for you:

   1 - litre of 40% (80 proof) alcohol
   15 grams juniper berries (bit less than ¼ cup)
   3 grams whole coriander, crushed (about 1 tbsp.)
   2 grams orange peel (about 1 tsp.)
   2 grams lemon peel (about 1 tsp.)
   1 grams whole cinnamon (about 1/2 stick)
   1 small cardamom pod, crushed

A tiny bit of Angelica would be another good addition, but it can be hard to locate (although I include a good source for herbs and additions in the Appendix). The ingredients above will be more easily available. Place the herbs into a large jar and add half of the alcohol. Place the jar in a dark, room-temperature spot for 3-5 days, and be sure to give the jar a good shake at least once a day. Add the rest of the alcohol and mix. Strain through a couple coffee filters. The mixture will have some colour. You can either live with the yellowish colour, or re-distil with a pot still so you get a clear gin with the tastes and aroma but not the colour.

If you intend to re-distil, I would make a larger volume, since making a small amount would be a lot of work in re-distilling for what you get. Also, when starting your steeping process, dilute the liquor a little, say with 20% additional distilled water just to provide a little more volume to the still. That additional water will be left behind after redistilling, so don't worry about watering down the product, but add the water at the beginning of the steeping process to keep the flavours and aromas throughout.

If you don't wish to redistill, as a compromise, you could use a filtering water jug (Brita for example) to help filter the liquid. You may have to run it through a couple times to get the desired effect. It may not clear it entirely, but will improve it. Gin generally is not aged in oak barrels, since it derives flavour from the ingredients. The disadvantage is that any filtering will remove some of the taste and smell of the gin. Not all, but it will be reduced (it is essentially carbon filtering the liquor)

To make a traditional gin from scratch in a larger batch, use sugar as a base and make a basic wash as outlined earlier. Then adjust the above ingredients for the quantity you are making (you can probably halve the amounts per litre, since they will be soaking for 1-2 weeks), and add at them at the beginning of the ferment, stirring once or twice a day. In other words, according to the above amounts, for 20 litres of wash, you would use 15 grams of juniper berries x 20 ÷ 2 = 150. So for 20 litres of wash, you would start with 150 grams of juniper berries. Do the same with the other ingredient quantities. Over the one or two week fermentation period, the ingredients will flavour the wash. Strain them out of the wash after fermentation before you pot distil. That way, you will get a clear gin with the taste and flavour you want.

Another method is to dilute your primary distillate (vodka or maceration) to about 35 - 40 percent abv. Then, redistill using a pot still with a tray suspended just below the mouth of the still. This tray should be copper or stainless steel, with holes or slots to allow the vapours to pass through it, and will contain the botanicals you wish to use to flavour your gin. I include a diagram for your understanding. A stainless steel steam basket for example would work just fine.

As the alcohol vapours evaporate and rise to the top of the still, they pass through the botanical tray and the goodness of the herbs and spices are absorbed into the vapour. This then provides the bouquet and flavour for your gin.

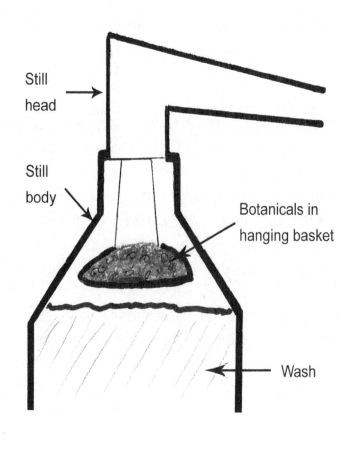

Still head

Still body

Botanicals in hanging basket

Wash

Again, you can vary the amounts of the above recipe, but this method will require more botanicals than will maceration (soaking), since they are exposed to the alcohol for less time, and it is a little less efficient process, although it will produce a clearer product than will maceration. By less efficient I mean that it will probably take a greater quantity of botanicals to produce the flavour and scent you want than maceration. Simply put, the alcohol is in contact with the botanicals for much less time than when macerating, so it may require more to achieve the result you want. You can use fresh or dried ingredients in the botanical tray. If you use dried, soak or wet briefly in water or alcohol to reduce the time needed to re-moisten and release their essence into the vapour.

Grappa

Grappa is Italian in origin, with equivalent liquors in France called 'Marc', in Spain 'Orujo' and in Greece, 'Raki'. It is distilled from the pressings of grapes used in wine production, the leftover pulp, skins, seeds, etc. This pulp, referred to as 'pomace', is fermented then distilled to make a sometimes-harsh flavoured liquor. Traditionally, it is served after dinner as a 'digestivo' to aid in the digestion of big meals! Generally, it is not aged, just made & bottled, although some higher-end Grappas are aged in oak.

Many people don't care for Grappa. It can be very strong and harsh. The harshness largely comes from the seeds and stems of the grape, so removing much of these from the pulp will yield a better quality liquor. White grapes will also be less harsh than red grapes, due to the fact that red grapes have more tannin in their skins.

To ferment, you will need pressed grapes, so if you make your own wine, you may be able to re-use your pressings to make Grappa. If not, ask a wine maker you know, or perhaps approach a winery about getting some of their pressings. This practice is not uncommon in some European countries.

I would add half the volume of the pressings in water, and some sugar to get the fermentation going. So, if you have 10 litres of pressings, add 5 litres of water, and a couple pounds (kilogram) of sugar. Again, use a good quality wine yeast, champagne or turbo yeast, and some nutrient if needed.

Ferment on the pulp (pomace) until sugars are used up (there should be no residual sweetness in the grape pulp or mash), stirring vigorously daily. Press out the liquid well and distil as you would any other wash. Most Grappas are between 35 and 50 percent alcohol by volume (ABV), or 70 to 100 proof.

Kirsch

Kirsch is a popular liquor in France, Switzerland and Germany, and is sometimes referred to as a type of schnapps. Made from ripe, sweet cherries, it is simple enough to make if you follow the directions.

Ingredients

- 15 kilograms (about 33 pounds) of ripe dark sweet cherries (stemmed and pitted)
- 6 litres of water
- 1 kilogram white sugar
- 20 grams Di-Ammonium Phosphate (available at wine/beer supply stores)*
- 15 grams Tartaric Acid (also available at wine/beer stores or possibly supermarket)*
- * If unable to find the last two ingredients, use the equivalent amount of yeast nutrient
- 1 packet of champagne yeast, turbo yeast (don't need nutrient if it's included in turbo package), or other good quality wine yeast.

Directions

- Mix all ingredients except yeast and cherries
- Boil, then cool to room temperature
- Aerate by beating or whisking for several minutes, then add yeast and cover
- Fermentation will start within two days
- When starter is actively fermenting, prepare pitted cherries as follows
- Crush or mash cherries well (wine press, wood mallet, food processor)
- Put in sterilized bucket/food grade container and add sugar wash
- Stir daily, ferment to dryness and strain out berries, pressing to get juice
- Distil in a pot still. Be sure to remove fore-shots, as they will be pungent
- If necessary, re-distil to achieve 40% ABV (80 proof) (or dilute if higher)

Rum

With traditional rum, the sugar comes from fermented juice of sugar cane, sugar cane syrup, sugar cane molasses or sugar cane by-products. Most is made in the Caribbean, Puerto Rico being one major producer.

There are three main styles of rum produced, white, amber and dark. The two former are light-bodied with dark being more full-bodied. Light-bodied rums are generally produced in column stills and distilled with an alcohol content of 80% or more. The spirit then spends at least one year in oak barrels. At this point, the rum is clear and normally designated 'white' rum.

Another type of light-bodied rum, aged in wood at least three years and, with caramel added for colour, is termed 'gold' or 'amber'. In contrast, full-bodied rums are made using a different process. Skimmings from previous distillations called "dunder" - are added to the molasses in fermentation vats. Fermenting it up to 20 days follows this. This 'must' is then distilled in pot stills, which retains more of its flavour and essences. This results in a very flavourful, aromatic spirit. Before bottling, this full-bodied rum normally requires at least five to seven years of barrel aging.

Obviously, all of this isn't practical for home production, unless you have access to sugar cane, barrels and lots of time.

To shorten the process, I use the following recipes to 'simulate' a variety of rums.

White rum - start with 500 ml (half a litre) of 40-45% alcohol.
- 1 - 20 ml bottle of white rum essence (Prestige or your preferred brand),
- 1 1/2 tablespoons of commercial light rum extract (from supermarket or bulk food store),
- 1 tablespoon of white sugar or high fructose syrup (also available from bulk food store). Use more if you like it sweeter
- Mix well (use some spirited shaking - pun intended!)
- fill the rest of the bottle to give you 750 ml. and shake again.

Amber rum - again, start with half a 1 litre bottle of 40-45% spirit.

    - 1 - 20 ml bottle of either white or amber rum essence.

    - 1 1/2 tablespoons of commercial light rum extract

    - 2 tablespoons of caramel syrup or flavouring (if caramel flavouring isn't sweetened, add 2 tablespoons sugar/syrup).

    - mix well and fill the rest of the bottle.

Dark rum   - half a litre of 40-45% spirit to start

    - 1 tbsp (½ of a 20 ml bottle) dark rum essence (I like Mörk Rom)

    - 3 tablespoons rum extract (from bulk food store/supermarket)

    - 2 tablespoons fancy dark molasses (not blackstrap)

    - mix well and top up to 1 litre.

Note that with the amber and dark rums, some settling can occur because of solids in the caramel and molasses. If it bothers you, just siphon or pour off the cleared liquor into a clean bottle.

Note also that when using molasses for flavouring, it may in time solidify. Very similar to honey in this way, you can simply heat it up to regain its liquidity, either in the microwave or in a hot water bath (put container in hot water, don't dilute it). Because of the high sugar content in both, they also keep exceptionally well without refrigeration.

These recipes are a starting point, and you may like more or less of a particular ingredient, depending how sweet or flavourful you like your rum.

Traditional method

If you want to try making traditional rum in a pot still, you can use brown cane sugar along with some dark <u>fancy</u> molasses (not blackstrap).
A good starting point would be:

   6 - pounds of dark brown cane sugar (as opposed to beet sugar)
   3 - pounds of molasses
   4 - gallons of water
   turbo yeast or yeast & nutrient

Heat three quarters of the water to about 140 degrees F. (or just use hot water) and dissolve the sugar and molasses. Add the remainder of cold water and when under 90 degrees F., add the yeast and nutrient. Cover and ferment until dryness. Distil in a <u>pot</u> still.

Don't be tempted to use all molasses, since this will make for a very thick wash, and will be more difficult to ferment and distil properly.

Although the must/wash will be dark in colour, it *will* distil mostly clear. If you want an amber or dark rum, you can refer to the above recipes and add some molasses, caramel colour, or essence to give that colour (and some of the flavour style) back in.

Aging in oak will also add some colour and will improve the flavour…if you can be patient enough!

If you like spiced rum, I include a recipe in the alphabetical recipe section.

Schnapps

Schnapps, a German word, is the generic term for white or clear brandies distilled from fermented fruits. True Schnapps has no sugar added and is definitely an acquired taste, particularly for nationalities not used to raw distillates. It is also known as eau-de-vie in France.

Schnapps differ from liqueurs in that they are both fermented *and* distilled, but liqueurs are often simply fruits steeped in alcohol or alcohol with fruit flavouring and sweetness added. True Schnapps is made from the start with fruit, distilled and no sweetness added to the final distillate. In many countries, the term 'schnapps' is used somewhat interchangeably with liqueur with both commonly sold as <u>sweetened</u>, flavoured liquors.

To make a true schnapps, one would need to ferment your chosen fruit as if you were making wine. Then, pot distil the must (with the fruit strained out) to retain the character of the fruit. It's totally possible to do with the methods I laid out, but it will take longer since you essentially have to make a wine *first*, and allow it to ferment to dryness (so all sugar is used). You may also choose to ferment the must on the fruit for a longer period of time in an anaerobic environment, to retain more flavour and aroma of the fruit. Also, the inclusion of the skins will often enhance the flavour and aromas of the fruit. With citrus fruit however, omit the bitter white pith.

Depending on the fruit, you may have to add some sugar to the fermentation process in order to attain a decent level of alcohol to distil. Sweet fruits such as apples may not require any added sugar, but other fruit such as elderberries certainly would.

This fermentation process will be a much longer process than the few days it will take to ferment plain sugar, and can take up to a month. It may however be a rewarding experience for you. It can also give you some experience making wine as well as distilling the final result. You may even like the wine enough to simply bottle and drink that!

Tequila

This is a tough liquor to make yourself the traditional way. Tequila is made from the Blue Agave plant, and produced in Mexico. There are strict regulations guarding both the name and production area of the liquor. So much so, that any other producers not in the controlled area of Mexico, and producing it from at least 51% Blue Agave, cannot call it Tequila. The difference between Tequila and Mezcal is that Mezcal can be made from any agave plant, where Tequila is only made from the Blue Agave.

The actual making of Tequila will be a daunting process for an individual. First, it takes up to 12 years for the plants to mature enough to harvest the liquid. Secondly, you will need quite a few plants to make any significant amount of alcohol. Third, only the heart or 'piña' of the plant is used. These can be 20 to 80 kilograms (50 to 175 pounds) each, and look similar to a large pineapple. They must be slowly cooked or roasted (up to several days) to break down the complex carbohydrates into sugars. Then they must be shredded, pressed and filtered. A very large oven is be required, plus equipment to press them. The roasting (at 175 to 205 degrees F.) softens the flesh, releases the sweet juices, and helps convert starches into sugars, which are then fermentable.

So, I suppose if you have a ready source of mature Blue Agave (it can take more than 10 years to mature), and large enough ovens, presses and equipment, you could go through all of this work. However...if it were me, I would use a good quality essence with your easy to make moonshine!

Another solution to making your own tequila is to use Blue Agave syrup, which is produced commercially. A recipe follows. The amount of agave syrup is adjustable, but the sugar content I recommend will total the 8 kg amount called for by turbo yeasts. I would recommend at least 5 kg syrup and 3 kg sugar, but the more syrup you use, the more 'authentic' product you will have.

Recipe:

- Pour 6 kg of Blue Agave syrup into your fermentation bucket as described in 'making a basic wash' section, Add 12 litres of boiling water and dissolve the syrup. Add 2 kg white sugar and mix until dissolved.
- Top up with cool water to 20 litres.
- Cool mixture to below 90 degrees Fahrenheit and add a package of turbo yeast, or packet of champagne yeast (add some yeast nutrient) and stir.
- Allow to ferment to dryness (5 to 7 days).
- Distil in a pot still, removing the first ounce or so of distillate (fore shots), which should give you a liquor of about 20-25% (40-50 proof)
- Re-distil the liquor, again removing the fore-shots.
- Take an alcohol reading and dilute to about 40% alcohol (80 proof) with distilled water.
- If you want amber tequila, add some oak chips for a couple weeks and let sit, stirring or shaking every couple days. Then, strain out oak chips and if necessary, filter through coffee filters.
- Bottle and enjoy!

Vodka

One of the world's most popular liquors, vodka is traditionally made from potatoes, grain or sugar beets and has very subtle or little flavour or aromas. Some companies actually ferment it the same way you will, with only sugar and yeast. So, you essentially have vodka already!

If you want to drink it straight up, you should consider double filtering your moonshine to give it the purest flavour possible. There are essences you may add that simulate the flavour and aroma of specific commercial vodkas, but you'll have to try them for yourself to see if you like them or indeed if it's even necessary. Filtering may be all you need!

Traditional Vodka recipe

- Scrub 20 pounds of potatoes clean, cut into chunks, (do not need to peel). If you wish, add one or two pounds of crushed wheat.
- Add enough water to cover in a large pot and boil until very soft.
- Drain water (but save it), and mash potatoes.
- Put into fermentation bucket and add boiled water, and enough good clean hot water (about 160 degrees Fahrenheit) to make 5 gallons.
- If using malted grain, add 2 pounds and mix well. If not using malted grain, add amylase enzyme and stir well.
- Let sit for 24 hours, stirring frequently (starches will convert to sugar).
- You can either strain it at this point, or ferment on the mash. I would ferment on the mash, since it continues to release sugars for a couple days into the fermentation. It is a bit messier, but you'll have to strain it regardless. The key to fermenting on the mash is to be sure to oxygenate the mash well…especially since it will be quite thick. Yeast needs oxygen to thrive, so stir it vigorously daily.
- Let cool to below 90° F, add yeast, and ferment to dryness.
- Strain mash, and it's probably best to let it clear a bit before distilling.
- Distil the wash (either a pot or reflux still). You'll want to achieve about 40% ABV (80 proof). (Remove heads and tails as previously described).
- Charcoal filter as described previously (if desired).

Whiskey

Whiskeys are largely made from cereal grains such as corn, rye, and barley to get their unique flavour. Commercially, to be labelled a particular type of whiskey, strict laws of content and aging must be followed. In the US, Bourbon, by law, must be between 51 and 79% corn and must be aged in new charred oak barrels.

Canadian whiskey is traditionally made mostly from rye grain, hence 'rye whiskey'. However, today it is many times made from corn, along with rye and lesser amounts of other cereal grains. It is aged a minimum of 3 years and may be blended with older whiskeys to achieve a particular flavour.

In the US, to be labelled a rye whiskey, it must be at least 51% rye grain. Irish whiskey is from malted and unmalted barley, corn, and lesser amounts of other grains, and also aged at least 3 years. Scotch is unique in that it uses primarily malted barley that is dried in kilns using peat fires, which also imparts a smoky flavour. Bourbon must be at least 51% corn to be sold in the US.

In any case, whiskies are aged for years in charred barrels (the inside is burned to impart flavour) or uncharred barrels to achieve their smoothness and flavour. You may also purchase barrels for home use, in various sizes and levels of charring.

The most common are American and French white oak and charring is available from none to a light toasting to deeper charring. These barrels are quite expensive, not to mention large, so unless you are familiar with the flavour you are seeking, and how to properly choose and use a barrel, I would stick to flavouring your alcohol using essences. You will be able to get consistent, repeatable results in much less time.

If you do want to use barrels, there are a couple things to consider. It would likely be better to get a lightly charred barrel rather that one with medium or heavy 'toasting' (another term for charring), simply because you can always age your spirit longer for more flavour, but if it becomes too strong as with a heavy charring, you'll be stuck with it. Also, you must take good care of your barrel. Because it is made of wood, a natural product, it will be subject to infections the same as you or me, or garden plants. Too moist an environment and mold could grow on it, too dry and it will crack.

That leads me to proper preparation of the barrel. You should sterilize the barrel when you get it with boiling water, then, fill it right up with distilled, pure water (no chlorine). You will need to expand the wood, which will swell with the water. Move it around a couple times to make sure water is on all sides. It may leak a bit at first, so don't use alcohol, because much of it may leak out, wasting your hard earned work. After the wood swells for a couple days, joints between staves will be very tight, and not allow any further leakage. Then drain the barrel and fill it with your alcohol.

Most commercial essences do a good job of simulating whiskey flavourings. I would invest in the best quality one offered. Prestige 'Legend' whiskey essence is excellent, but remember, this is largely my opinion and my personal preference (and I like rye whiskey). I also tend to mix them slightly stronger than recommended on the bottle to achieve maximum flavour. For instance, I tend to use 1 1/2 - 20 ml bottles of essence for 1 litre of spirit, which is slightly stronger than instructions give.

Another trick to impart an aged flavour to a whiskey is to add a couple spoonfuls of cream sherry to the flavoured spirit. Add a bit at a time and taste how it progresses. You can use dry sherry if you prefer not to add any sweetness, but a little sweetness will also help soften the flavour. Sherries are themselves heavily aged, and adding a little bit will impart that aged taste to your whiskey. Port also may be used…the result will be a bit fruitier than with sherry.

When making Scotch, there are more options to impart that smoky aged flavour. I hate to sound like a broken record, but I like the 'Ambrosia' scotch flavouring by Prestige. They also make oak chips for additional flavour.

For a scotch that is really convincing, add the liquid flavour according to directions, and then add half the amount of oak chips to the already flavoured liquor. Let this sit for 2 or 3 days, giving it a shake a couple times a day. Let it settle and filter it through a coffee filter into a clean bottle. This fooled a couple scotch drinking friends of mine when I gave them a taste!

There are other oak chips on the market, available at wine stores, which may also be good, but I find the combination of the two types of flavourings is the key.

If you like a really smoky flavour to your scotch, you can also add a small drop of Liquid Smoke found in supermarkets. Be VERY careful with this one though. It's a strong flavouring and could overpower the taste of your scotch. Another way to maximize the smoky flavour is to use half the liquid amount of Ambrosia flavouring, but the WHOLE package of Ambrosia, or other oak chips (according to directions of the manufacturer).

The Traditional Way

For those purists out there, who would like to try making their own traditional whiskey, I'll outline here some technique and some original recipes from some very well regarded sources.

The disadvantage of making your own spirits from scratch, using grains, is that it will be a lot more work for you. It will however, give you satisfaction in the end product to be able to say that 'you did it yourself, just like in the olden days', but be prepared for additional steps and equipment.

First of all, you need to cook these grains in order to release the flavours, starches and sugars from the grain, since this is what the yeast will consume to produce alcohol. The yield per gallon of mash will not be as high as with sugar, since there is a limited amount of sugar in the grain, compared to straight sugar. In order to cook this mash, you will need a vessel big enough to hold the water and the grains. You could use your metal still, but it will produce a mess and will be hard to clean out, and I really don't recommend distilling with the grains in the still. It will be prone to burning, and could not only wreck your run, but ruin your still.

So, you will need a rather large metal pot, large enough to hold the grains, and enough water to cook them. No need to cook the full volume unless you have a really large container, half or even one-third of the water volume would be enough. A large soup pot or stock pot would be fine. You need to heat the water and add your grains. You will need about a pound of grain to about 2 quarts or litres of water, so for 20 litres, you'll need about 10 pounds of grain. The ratio of grain types will be up to you and your taste, but should be about 1 pound to 2 litres of water, or 2 pounds per gallon. (If you're going to add sugar, you can cut these amounts in half).

If you don't have a pot large enough, you can reduce the amount of water you use to cook the grain to maybe 75% of the volume. Cook the grain in the water, then after cooking the mash, add the remaining water back in when transferring to the fermenting container. This will also help cool it faster too. However, it's still better to use the full amount if possible.

Buy the grains as cracked, rolled or milled grains, so you don't have to do it yourself! Cook it slowly between 160 to 180 degrees (Fahrenheit) to allow the starches to come out of the grains. Don't go above 180 degrees. You have to stir this regularly…<u>you don't want it to burn</u>. This starch will be converted to sugar and feed the yeast in later steps.

And, just to make things easier for you, heat the water first, then add the grains. You pretty much have to stir constantly to avoid burning the grain. Some grains will float, but some will naturally sink. If it's sitting on the bottom, nicely compacted and not stirred, it will burn and ruin your whole batch. So to save your arm muscles, heat the water, then add the grains and start stirring.

You can also use whole or cracked grain, but it will require longer cook times to release the starches. It's a bit messier to use meal, but it will cook and ferment faster, and release more of its carbohydrate structure. As I said before, it's a more complex process than sugar alone. If you don't want to deal with the messier ground meals or grains, at least use cracked corn or course ground or crushed grain. Whole grain would just take too long to cook down. The courser the grain, the longer it will take to cook it down.

Incidentally, it is normal for the mash to thicken when cooking grains. This is a result of the starches in the grain coming out. Be sure to use enough water as this mash thickens, so as not to burn it. The enzymes or malt you will add will lessen this thickness, as the starches are converted into sugar.

It is necessary to use some form of enzymes to your mix, either some kind of malted grain or commercially available amylase to add these important enzymes to the mash. These help convert starches to sugars, which in turn are consumed by the yeast. You can also sprout part of your grain, then dry and grind it. This process (malting) produces the enzymes you will need. Malted barley has one of the highest enzyme contents. Add the malt or enzymes to the mash after cooking the grain + cooling to about 150 degrees F. Higher temperatures will destroy the enzymes. Stir in well and let sit for a few hours to allow time for starches to convert to sugar.

You'll want to cook the grains for about 15 minutes at the higher temperature, then remove the heat source and allow it to cool to 150 degrees (Fahrenheit). This is when you will add your malted grain or enzyme. Stir it in for a few minutes and you'll see the thickness of the mash (from the starch) reduce and thin. This is due to the action of the enzymes in the malt converting the starch into sugars.

For argument sake, the grains we are talking about are dried grains. If you have access to fresh harvests such as corn, there's nothing wrong with using fresh corn. Common sense would say not to use the whole cobs obviously, but slice it off and mash it to open the kernels and release the juices. It will be a lot of work, but result in a lovely fresh flavoured whiskey!

To find grains, there are several sources. There are of course online suppliers, especially brewing specialty stores, but be aware that because of the weight of these, shipping may cost a pretty penny! I would suggest local sources such as a bulk food store at which you can usually order larger quantities. Natural food stores are also a good source, and carry organic product...it may cost a bit more to go all organic however. Another great source is farm supply outlets, such as a co-op (after all, animals also eat grain!). Actually, many moonshiners use an all-grain horse feed or 'sweet feed'. Co-ops and farm supply stores will also be able to supply large quantities and varieties of grains. Common sizes are 20 to 30 kg bags, and most will sell cracked or rolled grains, which will save you having to mill it. Be careful however, not to buy feed with additives. These may be meant to help farm animals, but may not be too good for your mash!

And, if you get really technical, when you're buying barley, '2-row' is better than '6 row'. The 'row' refer to how the grain grows...2-row has flat grain on each side of the stalk, 6-row has 6 heads around a central stalk. More importantly, 2-row is lower in nitrogen which results in fewer high or 'off alcohols', and a bit higher in starch. These rows are sometimes refered to as 'ears' also (as if there wasn't enough terminology already!!)

If you have to buy whole grains, you can 'grist' (crush or crack) them yourself with a bit of effort. Use a food processor, blender or even a rolling pin and a large zip lock bag to limit the mess, and crush the grain into small pieces. This will help get the most out of the grains. This will be harder to do with corn, so you should try to get it fresh, or pre-cracked.

In most cases, you may want to add some sugar to the heated mash…as a matter of fact, you will probably need to. For one thing, it will cost you a lot more to use grains alone, and you won't get as high an alcohol content to your mash using grains only. If you're a purist however, you can just stick to grains, it will just cost more and be more work!

How much sugar you add depends on a few factors. First is the kind of grain you use. Corn, rye and wheat are a little more fermentable at about 55 to 60 percent than oats and barley, which are about 45 to 50 percent fermentable. Secondly, it depends on the yeast you use. Higher yielding yeast will let you add more sugar and get a higher alcohol content. Third, it depends on how 'rich' a flavour you are going for. More grain will give a more flavourful distillate. If you use a lot of sugar, you will end up with a higher alcohol content, but you have to 'cut it' to a more drinkable level by adding water, which will also dilute the flavour to a degree. As a rough starting point, add a kilogram of sugar per gallon of mash for extra sweetness, and see how you feel about the result!

Let the mash cool to below 90 degrees F., and add the yeast. It will take between 5 and 10 days to ferment (depending on the yeast and temperature you're fermenting at). It will be done when you don't notice any more bubbles or 'head' on top, and it will not taste sweet, but have an alcoholic and perhaps slightly bitter taste.

Strain out the grains so you don't have solids in the still, which may burn. As I said earlier, you'll want to use a pot still to retain the flavours and fragrances (nose) of the alcohol. Also be aware that when using grains to ferment, that there will be more 'heads' or congeners early in the distillation. This was not as much of a problem using sugar, but you will notice these 'off alcohols' more with grains. The heads should definitely be removed as distillation starts. A few ounces probably, depending on the size of your run. You'll be able to taste the difference between the head and the 'heart' (the good stuff in the middle!)...the first alcohols smell and taste bad. Don't drink this, but use it for cleaning, charcoal BBQ starter fluid, alcohol lamps, or just throw it out.

Various types of whiskeys call for different amounts of grains, but the most common grains used are rye, corn and barley. Rye whiskey, as its name indicates is usually higher in rye grain. Bourbon however, uses more corn as its base and is slightly sweeter than rye. Other grains can be used, but these are the most common. If you don't want to malt your own barley (see next page), you can also use a malt extract, which is available from a wine or brewery supply store (it's commonly used in making beer. Be sure it is a diastatic variety...also called Bakers Malt). Buy the unhopped variety, and usually a light or pale works best. Like I said...the amounts of the particular grains will vary with taste, but you can decide what you like. There is nothing wrong with using corn entirely, and some people like a liquor made entirely with malt (such as Scotch). Some recipes follow the malting section, including a couple from two well-known characters of note.

So to summarize quickly;

- Use cracked or rolled grains in whatever combination you desire, about 2 pounds per gallon total grain. (Or half as much if you're using sugar too).
- Some of the grain content should be in the form of malted corn or barley (can be a small percentage, even 5% to 10% is OK.) Otherwise, use an enzyme such as amylase.
- Heat the water, add your main grains (not the malt) and cook for about 15 to 20 minutes at 160-180 degrees, depending on the density of the grains (corn may require more time than barley for example), stirring constantly.
- Remove heat and let cool to 150 degrees, and add malt or enzyme and mix well. Add sugar now also if you are using it.
- Let cool to below 90 degrees. Add yeast and stir well. Cover and let ferment for 5-10 days, stirring at least once daily, until no sweetness is tasted.
- strain solids out of mash and distill the wash.

Malting

Although it is much easier just to purchase malted grain from a brewery supply source, I will give directions should you want to do your own.

Barley is the most common and also one of the safest grains to malt. I wouldn't recommend you try oats or rye at home, since these grains *can* attract *butryfying* bacteria during the process, which could be harmful (these malt varieties are available commercially however). Corn is also acceptable. Use untreated grain, especially if choosing seed grain, and best if it's grown for use in brewing. It can be stored in a cool dry place in paper bags for up to several years. You can use either two-row or six-row barley, but six-row will produce more enzymes (2-row for higher starch content when fermenting).

To malt your own grain, use 10-20 percent of the weight of the grain you are using for making your mash. In other words, if you are using 10 pounds of corn in your mash, malt 1-2 pounds of corn or barley. If you know you will be using malted grain a lot, you can do a larger batch and keep it for future use.

Start by washing the grain (use a bucket, etc). Fill it with cold water and and stir. Most will sink to the bottom. Any unusable grain or debris will float to the top. Remove this and drain the water.

The grain must then be steeped in cool water (not icy cold, but cool at least). Cover the grain and stir/agitate well. Water must be changed at least 3 times a day. Soaking will take 2-3 days. The grain will have swollen to about 40-50 percent larger.

Now, the grain must be germinated. To do this, spread it on a cloth (an old sheet would work well). It must still be kept damp, and turned gently at least 3 times a day. The easiest way would be to spread the grain on half the sheet, fold it overtop, and lightly spray it to wet it down. Turning then simply involves flipping over the sheet and making sure the grain is still spread out. It will take anywhere from a few days to a couple weeks to sprout. It's also best if the room temperature is between 16 to 20 º C.

When the grain roots are nearly the length of the seed, it's done. Too short and the process isn't far enough along. Too long and the roots have started using the sugars in the seed.

You then need to dry it (kilning) as quickly as possible without scorching it. A dehydrator is fine, or an oven set low, between 50 to 70º C. Don't use too thick a layer, or it won't dry evenly and could scorch the seed. Too hot and it can destroy the enzymes you've worked so hard to achieve! You could even spread it into a thin layer on a clean sheet and put a fan on to gently air dry.

After dry, the rootlets must be removed. You can shake them in a lidded bucket or rub to remove them (they will add bitterness to the brew).

Finally, it's best to crush or grind the malted grain.

As you can see, this can be an onerous process, and can take quite a while to complete! However, if you do a large batch at once, the malt can be stored in paper bags, in a cool dark place, the same as the grain. Don't use plastic unless you are certain it is bone-dry, because any residual moisture will be trapped and it can mold or rot. It is a natural product and needs to breathe.

Historical Moonshiners

George Washington

Although not technically a moonshiner, one of the most highly regarded Americans, first president George Washington, was also one of the largest and respected whiskey makers of his time. Beginning in 1797, by 1799 he was producing 11,000 gallons of rye whiskey a year with five copper pot stills near his home at Mount Vernon, Virginia, on which he also paid tax.

Remember, back in those days, there wasn't much in the way of regulation! Many historical politicians and figureheads had businesses, which they were allowed to run freely. He also farmed and used the slop from the distillery to feed his pigs! Wouldn't they be happy hogs?!

At the time of his death in 1799, he also had apple, peach, and persimmon brandy, plain whiskey, and cinnamon whiskey in the Mansion's basement.

His rye recipe consisted of 60% rye grain, 35% corn and 5% malted barley.

The distillery has since been revived, and a few hundred gallons a year are made seasonally, and sold at a premium from the site.

Popcorn Sutton

A well-known Appalachian moonshiner was Popcorn Sutton who ran large stills in the back woods for decades. He did have run-ins with the law, and eventually was prosecuted for his passion. In 2009, after also having been diagnosed with cancer, he committed suicide at the age of 62 rather than spend time in federal prison for his conviction.

Although moonshine was and is illegal in the U.S., the well-known bootlegger left behind his recipe to produce the hooch, which a friend now legally produces and markets by calling it Tennessee White Whiskey. He published the autobiography 'Me and My Likker' in 1999.

Sutton's recipe:

> 25 pounds coarse ground white corn meal, enough to fill half of your barrel/container (*he preferred white over yellow corn*)
> 50 pounds of sugar - 1 pound of sugar per gallon of water of total volume *(which means he used about 50 gallons of water)*
> 1 gallon of corn malt (about 6 1/2 pounds) (*you can also use barley.*)
>
> Boil the water, cook the cornmeal and allow to cool to touch *(140-150 degrees)*.
>
> Add sugar and malt and stir in well. Leave for a day and come back. The mix should be bubbling on top, stir one last time and then leave it.

Obviously, he would have had a container large enough to house all these ingredients. If you don't…and you probably don't, just downsize the ingredients and quantities proportionally to fit your container(s).

Although backwoods moonshiners frequently say you don't need yeast, I would recommend the addition of a good <u>whiskey</u> yeast (not mentioned in Popcorn's recipe). There are natural yeasts present everywhere, but they are too unpredictable as to quality, strength and viability. They may brew too weak, or give off flavours to your mash. Better to use something known. But, but if you want to be true to his methods, you can try the recipe using your own malted, dried and ground corn malt.

He distilled this off with a large copper still on a fire, using a thump keg and cooling 'worm' in a barrel.

There is a movie about Popcorn on the internet…as of this writing, the shortcut is: <u>http://www.youtube.com/watch?v=Yp56sT66D1U</u>

If you don't find it, search his name on YouTube if you're interested to know more about him, there are lots of videos…he was a real character.

Hatfields and McCoys

Two of the most legendary families in the American south are the Hatfields and McCoys, whose real-life feud cost many lives about the time of the Civil War.

A US television series was made about the present day families and their attempt to set up a legitimate moonshine business together.

On one of the episodes, the families trade 'secret' closely guarded recipes in order to come together and make one brand, which will be commercially marketed.

The episode, which is available for download on the Internet, actually shows the recipe of the McCoy family, written on a piece of notepaper. I don't know whether or not it is the actual recipe, or just one used for television purposes (which I suspect, since I've seen an online page with a recipe that is almost word for word), but the recipe reads as follows:

For 5 gallons mash (19 litres):
- 5 gallons filtered water
- 7 pounds cracked corn (6-8 pieces or kernels is the proper crack)
- 7 pounds granulated sugar
- distiller yeast

It's a pretty basic corn whiskey recipe, which would work just fine, but in my opinion is still missing an enzyme ingredient in the form of malt or added enzymes. In this case, the corn would serve to flavour the mash, but wouldn't release much of its sugar since there is no component to convert the starch into sugar. This is called a 'simple mash', as opposed to a 'cooked mash', which is heated, the grain cooked, then malt or enzyme added. The sugar provides the majority of the alcohol content.

Whiskey grains

To get you started with fermenting traditional grains, I list some common whiskeys below with approximate amounts of grains.

Bourbon whiskey is largely a sour-mash (method follows in a few pages), and can vary widely, from 100% corn down to 65% corn. Traditionally, it would be 70 to 80 percent corn, 10-15% rye and the remainder, malted barley, perhaps 10-15%.

A rye whiskey would be at least 50% rye, 40% corn and 10% malt for example. Higher in rye would give you a more authentic brew.

An Irish Whiskey starting point would be 10 parts malted barley, 6 parts fresh barley grain, 2 parts fresh oats, 2 parts fresh rye.

Scotch malt whiskey would be 100% malt (often called single malt if from only one distillery). Note that true Scotch uses sprouted barley malt, dried over peat fires, which gives the liquor that distinctive smoky flavour. It is often distilled 2 or 3 times for maximum smoothness.

Another technique, which even commercial distilleries use, is to blend batches of whiskey. Lets say you made a batch that is a bit strong in rye… you can either live with it, or make another batch with much less rye, and blend the two together. Eventually, you'll settle on a recipe you like, but if you experiment and it doesn't work out entirely, blending can help save it! Also, an older batch of whiskey can be blended with a younger one to more rapidly help 'age' the younger one.

You may also find that there are variations of grains also. For example, there are many different varieties of corn, grown in many different regions. The type of corn you find in the southern USA may be completely different to that which you find in Europe, Australia, etc. This isn't bad, it just means that even if you follow a specific recipe, the flavour may vary slightly from region to region depending on the flavour of available ingredients.

It will take a little experimentation on your part to find the best combination of grains to satisfy your palate, but the recipes, ratios and quantities I've listed will at least give you a good starting point!

You will soon discover if you like a whiskey heavier in one grain or another. There is no right or wrong here...it will depend on your personal taste. Even commercial producers use various percentages of the various grains. No one recipe is better or worse than another...it's whatever you like! Common sense however says that if you want to make a corn whiskey, you would use a higher percentage of corn in the brew, same for rye, etc.

Again, when using grains rather than plain sugar, you will need to remove the first couple of ounces (or more for large batches) of distillate, which contain fusel oils and 'off-alcohols'. This is because there is more organic matter in grains that can ferment these unwanted by-products such as methanol. In any case, they should not be consumed.

For this reason, I don't recommend freeze distillation when fermenting grains, since these fore shots and tails cannot be removed by freezing.

Sour Mash Whiskey

OK, remember earlier in the book when I told you to discard the undistilled, leftover liquid after doing a run with your still? Well, sour mash whiskey is the exception to that rule.

It has its roots in the southern United States, and is a more complex, longer process to produce. It's used in most bourbons, and a legal requirement in Tennessee Whiskey.

The process involves re-using part of the spent grains and yeast of a previous batch of alcohol, along with part of the spent wash from the distillation process (also called the 'backset'). Spent mash is also called barm, stillage, spent beer, distillers spent grain, slop or feed mash, since it can be used as animal feed.

You may be familiar with the concept by comparing it to making sour-dough bread, which relies on using part of an earlier batch to start the next batch.

This process not only economizes by re-using yeasts...potentially and theoretically forever, but also ensures consistency between batches, provided you keep all the other ingredients the same.

There are a couple methods you can use. The first, a simple-mash method uses all corn, and involves no cooking of grains. The other, uses a combination of grains and cooking each time. I'll outline both methods.

Simple Mash Method

To begin, you need to produce 'sweet mash', which will be your originating fermentation. Since we won't be cooking the mash the corn will be mostly for flavour, and sugar will provide most of the alcohol. I'll refer to the recipe from the Hatfield-McCoy's above, since it is a good starting sweet mash recipe.

- To 5 gallons of filtered water, add the cracked corn (7 pounds), sugar (7 pounds) and yeast (about a tablespoon…whiskey or distillers yeast is best). I would also add a couple pinches of yeast nutrient.

- Fermentation should start within a few hours…a day at the most.

- Ferment to dryness until you see a layer of lees forming on the bottom. This could take 4 to 7 days, depending on the yeast used. (The mash should not taste sweet when done).

- Siphon off the wash at this point, just the liquid, no solids.

- Pot distill this wash, removing and discarding heads as usual.

Now you need to decide how much of the backset you will be using. Legally, to make most commercial sour mashes, a minimum of 25 percent is required, but I wouldn't use more than 50 percent. Let's round up amounts and say a good starting point is about 1 1/2 gallons (of your original 5). However, it will take some hours to distill the alcohol off and cool this 'backset'. So, after straining wash into still, in order to maintain the life of the yeast in the spent mash, add 3 1/2 gallons of water and 1/2 pound sugar to it and mix well right after siphoning. This will keep the remaining yeast alive until you are ready to add the backset after distilling.

OK, so your yeast is still happy and now you have your new alcohol and cooled backset.

- Reserve the alcohol (ok…maybe a few sips missing! ☺).

- Add 1 1/2 gallons of backset to your rejuvenated yeast and mash mix.

- Remove any spent, floating corn, and replace as needed (it will often last for 4 or 5 fermentations, but I would add at least 10 percent new each time just for fresh added flavour).

- Re-ferment this mash again as above, adding a pinch of nutrient also.

- When re-distilling, add the first run of alcohol back in. This will give it a more flavourful, authentic sour-mash flavour.

- For subsequent batches, the heads won't be as heavy, since much of the corn is being re-used. You can even save the heads and re-add them on subsequent runs.

- I would definitely keep the latter part of the hearts and the tails of the run and use them as feints (heads and tails re-used in subsequent runs). In other words, keep the last cup or two of each run and use it when distilling the next batch. This will also help maintain continuity of flavour from run to run.

Cooked Mash method

This method is not that much harder than above, except you will be cooking the mash each time before adding back with yeast. Use 6 pounds of sugar (not 7 as above, since more sugars will be converted from the grain by the malt). Also, in order to get a more 'complex' flavour, lets use a different combination of grains!

- Start with the same amount of water, but use 6 pounds of cracked corn, 1 pound of cracked or rolled rye, and 3/4 pound of malted barley.

- Cook corn and rye as in Traditional Method previous, and cool to 150°F. (If you don't have a large enough pot, you can use a bit less water...just add it back in with the sugar).

- Add malted barley to cooled mash and stir well. It should get less thick as the enzymes convert starches to sugars.

- Cool mash to below 90 degrees F., and add yeast & pinch of nutrient.

- Ferment to dryness, siphon off wash and distill, reserving alcohol.

- To maintain integrity of yeast, add half gallon of water back into the spent mash and yeast, along with 1/4 pound of sugar.

- Reserve 1 1/4 gallons of backset from the still run.

- Most of the grain will have been spent producing sugars for this wash, so I would strain out most of them, and start with a new batch of grains, cooking the corn and rye in 3 1/4 gallons of water.

- Cool to 150 degrees again and add malt.

- Add backset to mash, remaining sugar and re-add yeast mixture.

- Re-ferment, siphon wash and add alcohol from previous run.

- Re-distill and repeat process-preserving yeast.

Since you are using a lot more new grain than with the simple mash method, you may wish to discard most of the heads. However as before, I would definitely keep the latter part of the hearts and the tails of the run and use them as feints (heads and tails re-used in subsequent runs). In other words, keep the last cup or two of each run and use it when distilling the next batch. This will also help maintain continuity of flavour from run to run.

For both methods:

As I said previously, this process can be repeated almost forever if care is taken each time to preserve the integrity of the yeast. You may want to experiment with different yeasts for the first couple batches, just to see which you prefer (or do smaller test batches with different yeasts). Once you've nailed down your preferences, keep it going!

I've had much success in my winemaking by using a variety of different yeasts for different types of wine. You wouldn't use the same seasonings for different foods, why use the same yeast for every alcohol? Each will lend its own characteristics to your brew! Go online and see what's available for your area, or mail-order it from afar! There are yeasts made specifically for whiskey. Try a couple!

As I've said before...all of these recipes are just a starting point for you. Experimentation and doing it will teach you what you like and what you don't. Even commercially produced whiskies vary from company to company. You'll eventually settle on a recipe that you like!

And, it won't cost you near as much making your own!

You may decide you want less or more of the backset added to subsequent mashes. There's no rule set in stone...experiment and decide what is right for you! Remember though, when using backset, you want it as good tasting as possible, so be sure there are no solids in your still which might burn and lower the quality of the spirit and backset!

That's the basic idea. You can play around with different combinations of grains also. Most sour mash recipes are largely corn, but there is nothing to say you can't add different grains if you desire. Rye adds a spicier flavour for example. Many bourbons vary in the combination of grains used. Many also use wheat as opposed to barley.

Barrel aging will also benefit these spirits greatly, however, I've already covered that!

Fruit Liqueurs

With your base moonshine or ethyl alcohol, you can easily make a variety of fruit liqueurs or cordials simply by soaking your chosen fruit in moonshine or commercially available alcohol. This soaking is called maceration. For instance, if you wanted a banana liqueur, chop or mash a couple bananas, mix and cover with a litre of moonshine. Let soak for a week (in a closed container or jar, and preferably in the refrigerator), strain, let clear and add sugar to taste (1/2 to one cup per litre). The beauty of this is that you can still use the bananas! Spoon them on ice cream for a decadent dessert! This will work with nearly every fruit. Generally, you'll want between two and three cups of crushed fruit per litre of alcohol, depending on how strongly flavoured you want it, and how robust the fruit flavour is.

Even better than sugar is using a 'simple syrup'. The trouble with plain sugar added afterwards is that it doesn't dissolve as readily, and can make your liqueur a bit cloudy. Making a simple syrup, which is simply sugar added to hot water will make that much easier. The recipe is as follows:

Simple Syrup

You can make a thick, simple syrup using 2 parts sugar to 1 part water.

Heat one cup of water in a medium saucepan. Bring it to a low boil and add the sugar, stirring until dissolved.

Remove the syrup from the heat-source and cool.

Transfer the cooled syrup to a container or jar that can be stored in the refrigerator. Simple syrup can be stored for a couple months.

The great part of this is that you can use any fruit as a base to flavour your moonshine! Cherries, strawberries, oranges, lemons, raspberries, blueberries, apples, whatever. The quantity of fruit may vary according to how strongly flavoured it is, but as I said, you'll want at least 2 cups, and better is 3 cups per litre of alcohol, or even a bit more for a mild tasting fruit.

Use only good quality fruit, not rotten or shrivelled. If there are bad spots, cut them out. Wash or rinse the fruit first, as you would before eating it, just to be sure you wash off any dirt or impurities, then mash or chop up finely. I leave the skins on to give a bit of colour to the liqueur. The exception is citrus fruit where I zest the outside skin, peel the fruit and throw away the white pithy part of the peel, which is bitter. Along with the chopped fruit, this zest will greatly add flavour and colour to your drink. You can even use the zest alone from oranges, lemons or grapefruit. The zest from citrus fruits is very strong and will also give a great bouquet to your liquor.

Some fruits, such as melons will be much more subtle in taste and bouquet than stronger ones such as lemons, so like I said above, you may want to use a bit more fruit in that case (throw the melon skin and rinds away…they won't add anything to it).

Soak the slurry for between 1 and 4 weeks in the refrigerator, stirring or shaking each day to mix it all up. The length of time will depend on how strongly flavoured the fruit is. After you feel it's where you want it, strain off the liquor, press and filter it through a coffee filter or layered fine muslin. If it still needs clearing, let it stand a couple days and either siphon it off the sediment or pour it off carefully.

In order to help fruit liqueurs clear, it's important to understand the pectin content of the fruit. Pectin is what causes jam to gel with sugar and acid. But, the presence of pectin in your liqueur can keep it from clearing properly. Strange as it may seem, ripe fruit is generally lower in pectin than under ripe fruit.

Fruits highest in pectin are apricots, sour apples, bananas, blackberries and sour cherries, crab apples, cranberries, currants, gooseberries, grapes, loganberries, plums and quinces.

Medium pectin containing fruit includes sweet apples, ripe blackberries, sweet cherries, elderberries, grapefruit, peaches, lemons and oranges (and most citrus fruits).

Lowest are apricots, blueberries, figs, guavas, melons, pears, pineapple, raspberries and strawberries.

Now, in order to help your liqueur clear, I'm going to give you a winemaker's trick. Buy some 'pectic enzyme' at a local wine store, or online. It's cheap and will last for several batches. It basically causes the pectin in the fruit to break down and not leave a 'haze' to your alcohol. I add about a teaspoonful to a batch when you start soaking (best at beginning). Obviously, add less if it's a small batch and more if it's a larger batch. If you're only doing a liter or so, 1/4 teaspoon will be fine.

To sweeten the liqueur, add sugar or simple syrup to taste.

Another piece of advice…if you are using zest or peel from citrus fruit such as oranges, wash the fruit well before zesting, since there could be pesticides or wax on the surface (or even other people handling it). Who needs that added junk in your liqueur!?!

Also important is to use only the zest or peel of the citrus fruit, not the white pith, which is bitter and useless for our purposes. You can include the inside of the fruit and its juice if you wish. But believe it or not, you will get a great deal of the aroma and flavour of citrus fruit from the zest or peel!

Herbs and Spices

If you're into herbs and spices, you can also make concoctions of various ones: Cinnamon, coffee beans, dill, basil, thyme, peppercorns, hot chillies, vanilla beans, garlic or any other herb or spice you are fond of. Be careful how much you add however. Generally the spicier or more flavourful, the less you will need. Many people make oils and vinegars this way also.

Depending on the ingredient, they may also not need weeks to acquire their flavours. Often 2-4 days is lots, especially if you are adding them as an 'extra' ingredient. If it is your primary ingredient, then feel free to steep or age as long as you feel necessary. Often, and you'll see this in my recipes later, I will recommend adding a spice or herb at the beginning or just at the end of an aging period, just to give a hint of a flavour or aroma. Smell and taste them to decide when enough is enough.

You can even try combining flavours. For example, if you are soaking apples, you can add some cinnamon at the end, a day or two before straining, to give kind of an apple pie flavour and aroma! Maybe raspberry with the addition of a vanilla bean would, in a similar fashion, compliment each other. Use your imagination!

As gifts, you can even give a decorative glass bottle with an infusion in it. Leave some of what you are infusing in the bottle...such as a cinnamon stick, or sprig of thyme, etc. Make a nice label, and maybe use some twine rope to make a bow around the neck. It'll look very country and chic.

Using essences and extracts

One way to flavour your moonshine quickly is to use flavourings, often called 'essences', such as those offered by Prestige, as I have already said. There are literally dozens and dozens of options available. Another is to use commercially available extracts such as found in supermarkets or baking specialty stores. These are generally fairly inexpensive, and available in a wide variety of flavour options.

Want a Crème de Menthe? Buy some mint extract.
Want Cherry Kirsch? Buy some cherry extract.
Want Amaretto? Buy some almond extract.

As a starting point, you will generally use about 25-30 ml (1 1/2 to 2 tablespoons) of extract to a litre of moonshine, depending on it's strength of flavour. You may also need to sweeten it to taste, depending on the type you're making. Just use a little sugar or simple syrup as above until you're happy with the sweetness level. There is really no way I can tell you exactly how much, since people's taste vary so much. I've been making wine for many years, and I have friends who like a very sweet wine, and others who like it cheek-puckering bone dry. So, you might be happy with a quarter cup of syrup, or, you may like a cupful. Neither is right or wrong. It's your preference! If you're unsure, start with a small amount of sweetener, then increase it until you're happy. Remember, you can always add more, but you can't remove it once added!

Really, you'll have a blast discovering new flavourings and ingredients from things you may never have considered before.

A great source of flavourings is the mixed drink section of the supermarket. There are lots of choices such as daiquiri mixes, fruit juice concentrates (peach flavouring for example makes great peach schnapps), and a variety of flavourings which you can use to make assorted cocktails and liqueurs simply by mixing with your homemade moonshine! You can even use frozen juice concentrates…just don't water them down as much!

The exact mixing will depend on the concentration of the product, but given that most liqueurs are around 20% alcohol, a good starting point would be to mix them 50-50…50% moonshine with 50% flavouring concentrate. If the flavour proves too strong, use 1/3 flavouring, 1/6 distilled water and 1/2 moonshine, which will give a less strong flavour, but still retain 20% alcohol by volume. Even if you mix it and the flavour proves too strong, you can cut it using equal parts of distilled water and moonshine until the flavour strength is to your liking. You may also decide that 20% alcohol is too much for you…just add more distilled water and/or flavouring.

Whatever you are making, you may want to visit an import or dollar store and pick up some decorative bottles to make the presentation of your liqueurs a little nicer! There are wide varieties to choose from out there, in various colours. For example, wouldn't blueberry liqueur look great in a blue coloured bottle?! Same goes for lemon cordial in a yellow bottle, etc. You'll find long necks, big bottles, little bottles, etc. Make sure you consider how to close these bottles before you buy them. Sometimes there are not tops included with these. You can use corks for most bottles but you need to find the right size. Wine stores will sell them, or craft stores often have corks too. You can even add an extra touch by including a bit of whatever you made, in the bottle. For example, drop a few blueberries in the bottle of blueberry liqueur, or a curly strip of lemon peel in a lemon cordial, or a sprig of tarragon in the tarragon infusion!

Whatever you are making, it's usually best to let the liqueur or infusion age a couple or three weeks to mellow a bit. As with most things, age adds a bit of smoothness!

If you are good on the computer, you may even want to make your own labels for your creations. Adobe Photoshop is great, although is expensive and has a steeper learning curve. You can make a basic label in Microsoft Word by importing an image and adding type and a border. Go to a stationery or office supply store and look for peel and stick type paper, then you can trim them and stick them onto your bottles easily.

Basic flavoured liqueur recipe

This recipe is simply a <u>starting point</u> to make your own flavoured liqueur. Substitute any flavouring extract you wish (PURE extracts will always give better results than imitation!). Further recipes will give more elaborate ingredients and instructions for more complex drinks, but this recipe will allow you to make a wide variety of flavours quickly and easily.

Ingredients

- 1 cup sugar
- 3/4 cup water
- 1 cup moonshine, vodka or neutral spirits (80 proof - 40% ABV)
- 4 teaspoons vanilla or other extract

Directions

- In a saucepan, combine sugar and water. Bring the mixture to a boil, then reduce the heat to low and let simmer 5 minutes. Remove from heat and cool to room temperature.
- Pour alcohol and extract into the room temperature mixture. Pour the liquor into a sealable decanter; seal and store for at least a week before serving.
- Substitute other flavourings for vanilla extract for different flavours... eg...butterscotch, chocolate, coconut, etc. Depending on the flavour, you may have to adjust the amount up or down a bit. What I give is just a guideline. Some extracts are stronger than others.

Popular liqueurs

In the section following, I give several dozen recipes for making a great range of popular liqueurs. Some are quite simple, others quite complex and involved. It has taken me some time to develop these recipes, and I hope you enjoy them!

Some use hard to find ingredients, but in the Appendix at the back, I include a couple online herb stores/sites in order to help you find what you need. In the larger scheme of things, the recipe won't be harmed overly to omit the odd thing you may have trouble obtaining, especially for very small quantity ingredients. Or substitute something you may think will work!

As I said at the beginning of this book, if producing alcohol is illegal where you live, you can still purchase alcohol at your local liquor shop and use that to make these recipes. Most stores have plain grain alcohol (Everclear is one trade name), or Vodka works also.

As with anything, feel free to modify these recipes according to your taste. Everyone is different, and as I've said before, there is no right or wrong. This is supposed to be fun, and part of the fun is experimenting with flavours to find what you like. These recipes are a good starting point however, and will help you achieve results, which I think you will appreciate!

You can also halve or double these recipes as needed. I made some recipes larger (such as apple pie moonshine) because, bottled with a nice label, they make good gifts!

So pick one you think you'll like, and try it! Then have your friends over and impress them too!!

Absinthe

Absinthe is one of those liquors that has a checkered past, full of legend and inuendo. Banned in the early 1900's by many countries, it was alleged to cause hallucinations, and was dangerous. That was due mostly to the fact that people drank it straight, and at 130-150 proof, it wouldn't take much to get one drunk! (A higher proof is required to extract flavours from herbs used).

Absinthe is one of the liquors that has a strong licorice flavour, but is complex in that you can use a variety of other herbs and spices to 'finish' it, and indeed, there are many variations of this drink. It was the drink of choice for many famous people in the past, including Van Gogh, Picasso, Degas, Ernest Hemingway, Mary Shelley and Oscar Wilde.

It can be made two ways, the best and most common being re-distilling after maceration. The second is simply to macerate and skip the extra distillation. This is more commonly called 'wormwood bitters', since without the additional distillation, it will be much more bitter. The main ingredients in most varieties of Absinthe are wormwood, anise, and fennel.

Ingredients

- 1 litre 65-75% (130 to 150 proof) moonshine or grain alcohol
- 1 1/2 ounces (about 45g) wormwood (*Artemisia absinthium)*
- 1 ounce (30g) Anise seed
- 2/3 ounce (20g) Fennel seed
- 1/2 ounce (15g) Chinese Star Anise (not Japanese…it's poisonous!)
- 1/3 ounce (10g) Lemon balm
- 1/4 ounce (7g) Hyssop
- 1 teaspoon (3.5g) Coriander seed
- 1/2 teaspoon (2g) Calamus root

These are the ingredients for the primary maceration, before re-distilling. If you wish, other ingredients you can consider are a pinch of the following: Veronica, Cardemom, Thyme, Mint, Sage, Angelica Root.

Directions

- grind all ingredients together.
- seal & macerate in a cool dark place for 3-5 weeks, shaking occasionally.
- strain out herbs…you will have a brownish, cloudy, fairly bitter alcohol.
- redistill the alcohol to clear and remove bitterness with a pot still. (You may wish to add a bit of distilled water to the alcohol, simply to avoid running the still dry. The alcohol will be separated out.)
- now comes a re-maceration with smaller amounts of the herbs.
- also, if you want a particular colour of absinthe (most are green, but there is also red), use herbs to impart the colour, or a few drops of food colour .
- green absinthe can be made green by using petite wormwood (*Artemisia pontica*), which is less bitter, green anise seeds and mint leaves.
- red absinthe can be made by excluding green herbs (except wormwood) and using spanish paprika, or another paprika you are fond of.
- use much smaller quantities of the herbs…concentrating on the primary wormwood, anise seed and fennel, with pinches of other herbs as desired.
- macerate for much less time…days, not weeks. Taste to see when it meets your liking, then stop. Too long and it will get bitter again!
- strain and allow to clear, siphoning off the clear liquor.
- bottle and enjoy.

Hint: If you are a really enthusiastic absinthe drinker, it might be handy to make separate macerations of the final ingredients…such as a small amount of 'petite wormwood liquor', 'anise seed liquor', 'fennel liquor', etc. Then, you can easily add small quantities of each of these liquors to your second distillate without having to macerate and wait for it to clear again. Given the complexity of this recipe, it may also be more practical to make this in larger batches than just a single bottle!

Serving: Since you will end up with absinthe that is between 100 and 150 proof, you would normally add water to the liquor. It would be too strong to drink at 150 proof! If properly made, you will get louching (cloudiness), which comes from oils present in the anise and fennel seeds. As follows:

Traditionally, a shot of absinthe would be added to a glass with an absinthe spoon and a sugar cube placed across its top. Then ice water is slowly dripped onto the sugar cube, which slowly dissolves. As the water and sugar are added, you will notice the cloudiness form...that is called louch or louching. The amount of water to add is up to your taste, but usually about two to three times as much water as absinthe is normal.

Search the internet for how to serve absinthe if you want more information.

Amaretto

This makes a very smooth, enjoyable version of amaretto, somewhat like DiSaronno.

Ingredients

- 1/2 cup white sugar
- 1/2 cup dark brown sugar
- 1/2 cup corn syrup
- 1 cup water
- 1 1/2 tablespoons almond extract
- 1 1/2 teaspoons vanilla extract
- 2 cups of 50% (100 proof) alcohol or moonshine

Directions

- Heat the water to a low boil in a saucepan on the stove.
- Add both sugars and corn syrup, stirring constantly until dissolved.
- Lower heat and simmer until it thickens slightly (5 - 10 minutes)
- Remove from heat for 15 minutes and add almond and vanilla
- Let cool to room temperature and add alcohol
- Mix well and bottle.

Anisette

Anisette is another of the licorice-flavoured liquors, such as Ouzo, Absinthe, and Pastis. There are variations with all of them, Anisette being primarily made with anise seed, or aniseed. It is also usually a bit sweeter than the other liquors.

Ingredients

- 1 litre moonshine, vodka or grain alcohol 80-90 proof (40-45%)
- 1 1/2 ounce (45g) of green anise seed
- 1/2 ounce (15g) fennel seed
- 1/3 ounce (10g) coriander seed
- pinch or two of fresh or dried mint leaves
- simple syrup to taste (probably 1/2 to 1 cup)

Directions

- grind or crush herbs together.
- add to alcohol and seal in a food grade container.
- let steep for 2 - 4 weeks in a cool dark place.
- strain or filter out herbs and let stand until clear.
- add simple syrup to taste.
- bottle and enjoy!

As with many recipes, feel free to make it your own by adding a pinch of other herbs you might like, such as cinnamon or lemon balm!

Apple liqueur

This liqueur will vary in flavour according to the variety of apple you use. Some are sweeter than others, so adjust the sugar/sweetener according to your taste. It will also vary in colour...red apples will be a pink or reddish hue, yellow apples, yellower, etc.

Ingredients

- 3 pounds of washed apples, chop and core, but leave skins on
- 1 1/2 litres of vodka or moonshine
- 2 cups more or less of sugar or simple syrup

Directions

- Core and chop apples leaving skins on
- Put in large enough jar or container and add alcohol
- Age in the refrigerator for 3 to 4 weeks, shaking regularly
- Strain and filter as required
- Add sugar or simple syrup and mix well

Variation:

- For more of an 'apple pie' taste, add a cinnamon stick, a whole clove and a pinch of nutmeg a couple days before the end of the steeping period. They won't require a month to infuse their flavours. Too long and it may become overpowering. Strain them out before bottling.

Apple Pie Moonshine

Apple Pie Moonshine is one of the most famous and popular drinks in North America, especially the Southern United States. It is more of a cordial than a hard drink, but is easy to make and quite delicious!

Ingredients:

2 liters apple juice
2 liters apple cider (sweet cider, not alcoholic)
2 liters moonshine (80-90 proof)
1 1/4 cups brown sugar
3/4 cup white sugar
4 Cinnamon Sticks
1/2 teaspoon ground cinnamon
1/2 teaspoon vanilla extract or 1 vanilla bean (optional)

Directions:

- Pour the apple juice and apple cider into a large pot
- Bring to a simmer on the stove
- Add sugars, ground cinnamon and sticks, vanilla (if desired), and stir.
- simmer for 8 to 15 minutes (longer will add more cinnamon flavor)
- cool apple juices and strain through cheesecloth or coffee filters to remove solids
- add the moonshine and stir well.
- bottle and enjoy

Note: This can make an excellent Christmas gift bottled in traditional mason pint jars with a fancy label and some rope or ribbon around the top!

If you want a stronger drink, simply use more alcohol, or a higher proof moonshine or neutral alcohol, which will make the end result stronger also.

If you want an extra strong apple flavor, mix in a few spoonfuls of undiluted frozen apple juice concentrate from the supermarket. It will boost the apple flavor considerably, without watering it down.

Apricot Liqueur

This is a very nice liqueur, best made from fresh apricots to get the best, most fruity bouquet. You *can* use dried fruit, however it won't smell quite as fruity.

Ingredients

- 4 cups fresh Apricots or 2 1/2 cups dried
- 1 litre Vodka or Moonshine
- 2 1/2 cups sugar
- 1/2 cup water for fresh, 1 cup for dried

Directions (fresh)

- Wash fresh apricots and pit them (some varieties actually contain minute amounts of cyanide in the pits or kernels. Probably not enough to hurt you, but why chance it. Some pits may be bitter, also undesirable.)
- Add the sugar and mash into fruit until dissolved
- Put into a sealable container and add alcohol
- Allow to sit for at least a month refrigerated or in a cool dark place, shaking or stirring a couple times a week.
- Strain out fruit and press to get juice
- Allow to settle, and siphon or carefully pour cleared liqueur off
- Add water to bring to 20% ABV, and bottle

Directions (dried)

- Cut up dried apricots into pieces and add water to soak for a couple days
- Do not drain any remaining water, but add sugar and mix until dissolved
- Add alcohol and age for at least 6 weeks, shaking or stirring twice a week
- Strain out fruit and press to get juice
- Allow to settle, and siphon or carefully pour cleared liqueur off of lees
- If needed, add a bit more water to reduce to 20% ABV, and bottle

Aquavit

This is a traditional Scandinavian drink usually served ice cold. For another caraway recipe, see Kűmmel.

Ingredients

- 2 tablespoons caraway seeds
- 2 or 3 cardamom seeds or a pinch of ground cardamom
- 1/2 teaspoon dried dill
- 1 litre of Vodka or Moonshine

Directions

- Crush caraway, cardamom seeds & dill and put in a sealable container
- Add alcohol and shake well
- Let sit for 3 - 4 weeks and shake a couple times a week
- Filter through coffee filter(s)
- Bottle

Banana Liqueur

If you like bananas, you'll love this liqueur, with a sweet banana flavour and scent! You can use Vodka or moonshine. For a more 'tropical' version, try using a light rum!

Ingredients

- 2 large ripe bananas, peeled
- 1 litre of vodka, moonshine or light rum
- 1 1/2 cups white sugar
- 3/4 cup water
- 1/2 vanilla bean (optional)

Directions

- Mash peeled bananas in a sealable container
- Pour alcohol on immediately to prevent bananas from turning brown
- Dissolve sugar in hot water & allow to cool (or use simple syrup instead)
- Mix with banana and alcohol and seal
- Age at least 3 weeks in refrigerator or dark cool place, mixing regularly
- If using vanilla bean, slit open and add a couple days before straining
- Strain off solids from liqueur and allow to settle a couple of days
- Siphon off cleared liquor or if needed strain through coffee filters.
- Repeat if necessary
- If desired, add a little water to bring to 20% - 25% ABV
- Bottle and enjoy!

Blueberry liqueur

This is delicious with fresh blueberries, but frozen works equally well (they're easier to breakdown due to the freezing process)

Ingredients

- 3 cups fresh or frozen blueberries

- zest of 1/2 lemon

- 3 cups vodka or moonshine

- 1 1/2 cups sugar or simple syrup

Directions

- Mash blueberries in a bowl, adding sugar until dissolved

- In a sealable jar, add blueberries, lemon zest & vodka or moonshine

- Mix well, seal the jar tightly and refrigerate

- Shake well every day or two and let steep for 4 to 6 weeks

- Strain out solids and let stand a couple of days

- If necessary, filter liqueur through coffee filter(s)

- Bottle & enjoy!

Butterscotch Schnapps (liqueur)

Not a true schnapps at all, but commonly called that, it is still a yummy recipe, and great drizzled on ice cream!

Ingredients

- 330 g (1 and 1/3 cups) brown sugar
- 60 g (1/4 cup) unsalted butter
- 170 ml (2/3 cup) light or golden corn syrup
- 1 tsp vanilla extract
- 1 litre (quart) moonshine or vodka
- 1 tsp glycerine (smoothes the liqueur)

Directions

- Combine the sugar, corn syrup and butter in a heavy saucepan
- Bring to boil, stirring constantly, over medium heat
- Turn the heat to low. Cook without stirring until soft consistency reached
- DO NOT overcook! It won't take long!
- Cool it, add vanilla, glycerine and alcohol and mix well
- Put in large bowl and refrigerate
- A layer of fat will form on top (from butter)
- Skim it off and bottle the cleared liqueur

Chambord

Chambord is a delicious raspberry liqueur made in France with mostly black raspberries, but also red raspberries as well as currants and blackberries, with notes of spices also. Below is a recipe approximating the real thing! A bit more complicated to make than some, but worth it!

Ingredients

- 3 cups black raspberries
- 2 cups red raspberries
- 3/4 cup blackberries
- 1/4 cup black or red currants (optional) or 3 tbsp Ribena syrup
- 2 cups acacia honey if you can find it - any light honey is ok too
- 1/2 of a cinnamon stick
- 1 whole clove
- 1 whole vanilla bean
- 2 litres of vodka, moonshine or best…brandy (if you've made it)
- 1 cup white sugar or simple syrup
- 2 cups water (or just enough to make it 18-20% alcohol by volume)

Directions

- Crush all berries and put in a sealable container large enough for all ingredients. (recipe can be halved if quantity is too great).
- Stir in the alcohol.
- Heat one cup of water and dissolve the honey & sugar/simple syrup.
- Let cool and add to container.
- Soak in refrigerator for 6 - 8 weeks, shaking or mixing regularly.
- 2 or 3 days before you strain it off, add vanilla bean, cinnamon & clove. The idea is to give it just a hint of the spice. If you put them in at the beginning, they would eventually be overpowering. Mix and taste daily and remove them when you feel it is time, or soak longer if desired.
- Strain off the solids, gently pressing berries to remove juice, and if needed, filter liquor through coffee filter(s).
- Add water if needed to dilute to 18-20% ABV (use alcoholmeter).
- Bottle and enjoy!

Cherry Liqueur

This is very similar to the Danish liqueur **Cherry Heering**. The only difference is that I recommend removing the pits from the cherries, since they contain trace amounts of cyanide, especially if cracked or broken. Probably not enough to hurt you, but why take the chance! They were originally included to give a slight almond flavour to the liqueur, but extract works too! If you opt for the old way, leave pits intact, don't crush them.

Ingredients

- 2 pounds (just under a kilogram) dark Bing cherries or dark red sweet cherries, pitted
- 2 cups white sugar
- 2 cups vodka or moonshine
- 2 cups brandy (or use all vodka or moonshine if brandy is unavailable)
- 1/2 teaspoon almond extract

Directions

- mash cherries with sugar until sugar is dissolved
- place into a sealable container and add alcohol and almond extract
- mix well and seal
- keep in cool dark place or refrigerator
- let age at least 8 weeks, shaking or stirring at least twice a week
- strain off cherries and press to get juice (can use them on ice cream…yum!)
- Let sit a couple days to clear and siphon cleared liqueur off of solids
- Bottle and enjoy!

Choco Maple Nut

This is similar to the Amaretto recipe, but making a luscious maple syrup and chocolate liqueur with a touch of hazelnut. Yummy!!

Ingredients

- 1/2 cup white sugar
- 1/2 cup dark brown sugar
- 1/2 cup maple syrup
- 1 cup water
- 1/2 cup cocoa powder
- 1 teaspoon hazelnut extract
- 2 cups 50% (100 proof) alcohol or moonshine

Directions

- Heat the water to a low boil in a saucepan on the stove.
- Dissolve the cocoa powder, stirring well.
- Add both sugars and maple syrup, stirring constantly until dissolved.
- Lower heat and simmer until it thickens slightly (5 - 10 minutes)
- Remove from heat for 15 minutes and add hazelnut extract
- Let cool to room temperature and add alcohol
- Steep in a sealable container for at least 2 weeks, shaking regularly.
- Let settle until clear, then filter through coffee filter(s), careful not to disturb sediment.
- Bottle and enjoy!

Coffee liqueur

There are a lot of variations you can make...I include a couple versions for you, but feel free to experiment, adding ingredients that you happen to like. Instead of vanilla, you could add almond extract for instance.

Ingredients

- 4 cups brown sugar

- 3 cups water

- 1/2 cup instant coffee granules

- 2 teaspoons vanilla extract

- 1 litre vodka or moonshine

Directions

- Heat the water in a saucepan or pot

- Dissolve the brown sugar and coffee granules and bring to a boil

- Simmer for 10 - 15 minutes

- Cool, then add vanilla extract and alcohol

- Bottle and enjoy (either by itself or added to coffee)

- This will make about 2 litres, but recipe can be halved.

Coffee Liqueur 2 (similar to Kahlua)

Ingredients

- 2 cups water
- 2 cups white sugar
- 1/4 cup brown sugar
- 1/2 cup instant coffee or 1 cup ground coffee
- 2 cups Vodka or Moonshine
- 1 small vanilla bean sliced open
- 1 tablespoon thick caramel sauce (like bakery caramel)

Directions

- Boil water and add sugar and caramel sauce stirring until dissolved
- Remove from heat and add instant coffee or ground coffee and stir well
- Add vanilla bean and allow coffee to steep for 20 minutes
- Strain coffee grounds out and allow to cool
- When cool, add alcohol
- Bottle

Cranberry Liqueur

This is an excellent liqueur to serve at holidays, as a top off to your roast turkey or goose dinner!

Ingredients

- 4 cups cranberries
- 2 cups Vodka or Moonshine
- 2 1/2 cups white sugar
- Zest of 1/2 a sweet orange or tangerine (no white pith)
- 1/2 to 1 cup water

Directions

- Pick off any stems from berries, and remove any bad berries
- Coarsely grind the cranberries (blender or food processor)
- Mash the sugar into the berries with 1/2 cup water
- Place into sealable container
- Add alcohol, orange zest
- Seal and age at least 8 weeks
- Strain off solids and filter through coffee filters
- If desired, add more water to adjust alcohol volume
- Bottle

Crème de Cacao

Ingredients

- 2 cups (500 ml) of water
- 1 1/2 cups of granulated sugar
- 80-90 grams of hard cooking semi-sweet chocolate
- 1/2 cup of unsweetened cocoa powder
- 2 cups (500 ml) of vodka or moonshine
- 1 tablespoon of vanilla extract
- 1 teaspoon light rum extract
- 1 teaspoon instant coffee (optional)

Directions

- Heat water in a saucepan and dissolve cocoa powder, sugar and coffee powder.
- In a small cup or double boiler, melt solid chocolate slowly, so as not to burn.
- Add melted chocolate to saucepan and stir well until melted.
- Cool mixture to room temperature or just above.
- Add extracts and alcohol and mix well.
- Put in sealable container and store for 3-4 weeks, shaking regularly.
- Allow to sit another couple weeks until sediment from cocoa settles.
- Without disturbing sediment, strain through coffee filter(s) and bottle.

Crème de Cassis

This liqueur is made from black currants and is very popular in France where more than 16 million liters are produced annually.

Ingredients

- 2 cups blackcurrants
- 2 cups sugar
- 1/2 cup water
- 3 cups (about 750ml) 40% vodka or moonshine

Directions

- Crush the blackcurrants and mix in sugar, adding some water if needed
- Put in a sealable container large enough for all ingredients
- Add alcohol
- Age for at least 8-12 weeks in a cool dark place
- Strain solids out and let liquor clear for a few days
- If needed, filter through coffee filter(s)
- Add water to bring alcohol content to about 20 percent

If you don't want to go through all the fuss or time of doing it this way, you can use Ribena syrup, available in many supermarkets. The concentration will be to your taste, but about 1/3 syrup, 1/6 water and 1/2 alcohol will give you a 20% alcohol liqueur that is very rich tasting! Make as much as you want with these proportions.

If you are fond of spices, you may also add some cinnamon, allspice and cloves for a little more depth of flavor. I'd keep it pretty light, maybe half a cinnamon stick, a couple whole allpice and a couple cloves. Add these 2 or 3 days before straining.

Crème de Menthe Liqueur

This is an old traditional favorite that can also be used in cooking or baking. The recipe below will give a nearly clear liqueur, but food coloring can be added for a festive touch. Green is most common, but if you want, you can make it any color you want, and create your own inventive name for it!

Ingredients

- 3 1/2 cups white sugar
- 2 cups water
- 3 cups vodka or moonshine
- 1 generous tablespoon of mint or peppermint extract
- 1 tablespoon glycerin (optional)

Directions

- Bring water to a boil, dissolving sugar while stirring constantly
- Let sugar water cool
- Add extracts and alcohol
- Stir in glycerin if desired
- Bottle and age for at least a couple weeks

Note: Be very careful when adding food coloring, not to add too much at once. To make a good green color, start with 4 drops of green and 1 drop of blue. Add a bit more if necessary to get your desired hue.

Curaçao

Curaçao is an island in the Caribbean, which this drink is named after. On the island grow Valencia oranges, called larahas there. Distilled clear, it is often coloured orange, blue, red or yellow.

Ingredients

- 6 Valencia oranges, zested (no white pith)
- 1 litre 40-45% vodka or moonshine
- 2 cups white sugar
- 1 cup water
- 1/4 cup orange juice
- 2 whole cloves
- 1 cinnamon stick
- 1 teaspoon coriander seeds
- if needed, few drops of orange vegetable colouring

Directions

- Zest the orange peel thinly (don't leave any white pith)
- Put into a container big enough to hold ingredients
- Add alcohol and orange juice to the zest and seal container
- Steep together for 3 weeks until colour is well out of zest
- Shake daily for the first week, then at least twice a week
- Near the end of the steep time, add cloves, cinnamon and coriander to the container for 2 days
- Strain all solids
- Boil water and dissolve sugar
- Cool and add to alcohol
- Add colouring if desired
- Let settle and if required, filter through coffee filter(s)
- Bottle

Drambuie

The origin of Drambuie is lost to time, but it is a Scottish liqueur, made largely from Scotch and honey, with some added herbs. The name hails from Gaelic, and roughly means "the drink that satisfies". The recipe calls for scotch, so either make your own scotch according to my previous recipe above, use a scotch essence in your moonshine, or go buy some!
Drambuie is 40% alcohol by volume, so if you want a 'true' strength, make a scotch at 50% abv, and the end result should be close to 40%.

Ingredients

- 750 ml (3 cups) Scotch whiskey (50% abv)
- 1 1/4 cups clear light honey (Heather is best…Scottish you know!), but clover works too
- 2 teaspoons dried Angelica root, chopped
- 1 teaspoon fresh rosemary leaves, chopped
- 1/4 teaspoon fennel seeds (crushed)
- 1/2 stick of cinnamon (abt 3 inches), broken up
- 4 inch slice of lemon peel (no white pith)
- pinch of mace

Directions

- put Scotch whiskey in sealable container
- warm honey (microwave?…don't boil), and stir into Scotch
- crush or chop herbs and add to mixture, along with lemon peel
- mix or shake well
- remove lemon peel after 2 days
- shake each day for 1 week total
- strain out herbs/spices with coffee filter(s)
- allow to clear if needed, and strain off clear liqueur
- bottle

Elderberry Liqueur

Elderberries grow wild in many areas of the world. The best ones to use are the black varieties (*Sambuca Canadensis or Sambucus Nigra* for example). They are not a sweet fruit but have a powerful flavour, and are very nutritious, rivalling grapes in their overall goodness. Some even credit elderberries with having preventative health benefits. Be sure to only use the dark black ripe fruit. Green fruit and plant parts can be mildly poisonous!

Ingredients

- 4 cups ripe black elderberries, washed and stemmed
- 2 cups Vodka or Moonshine
- Zest from 1/2 a lemon (no white pith)
- 2 cups sugar
- 1/2 cup warm water
- 1 teaspoon Glycerine (optional)

Directions

- Gently crush elderberries, add water & combine with sugar until dissolved
- Put into sealable container and add alcohol and lemon peel
- Age at least 3 weeks, then strain fruit and peel off and discard
- Filter through coffee filter(s)
- Stir in glycerine if desired
- Bottle

Grand Marnier

Grand Marnier is one of those liqueurs that are both very popular and historic. I believe the first Grand Marnier was made in the 1820's. The recipe is a closely guarded secret, as are many! The oranges used are citrus bigaradia, which is a bitter but particularly fragrant fruit. The company harvests it green and the outer peel is dried in the sun to preserve optimal aromas. For a liqueur, it is also much higher in alcohol at 40%.
Here is my close approximation:

Ingredients

- 4 bitter oranges (of course citrus bigaradia are best if you can find them)
- 4 sweet oranges
- 1 litre of 45-50% brandy or moonshine
- 1 1/2 cups white sugar (less if you are using a sweetened brandy)
- 1 teasp. vegetable glycerine (optional) - gives a smooth mouth feel

Directions

- Zest skins from all oranges, careful not to get bitter white pith
- Peel, juice & pulp the <u>sweet</u> oranges - without the white pith (do not juice the bitter ones - use them for jam or something else, but not this)
- Grind or muddle orange peels and with a pestle or wooden spoon, grind the sugar into the peels
- Put peels and sugar mixture in a sealable container
- Add sweet juice, sweet orange pulp and the alcohol
- Mix well and seal
- Refrigerate and steep for at least 8 weeks, 12 is better, shaking a couple times a week
- Strain off the solids and let the liquor settle undisturbed for a few days
- When it clears, filter the cleared liquid through coffee filter(s), taking care not to disturb any sediment at bottom.
- Bottle and seal. If you use slightly higher alcohol (45-50%). This liqueur should work out to about 40% ABV, allowing for dilution from the juice.

Honey liqueur

There are a wide variety of honeys in the world, depending on the type of plants and region. Clover honey is one of the mildest and most common varieties and is sold in many grocery stores. Pick a variety you like then decide if you want to use additional flavors like orange zest and cinnamon when making the syrup. This recipe uses a neutral spirit like moonshine or vodka, but if you would like to substitute another spirit such as whiskey or rum, you may want to use slightly less honey to allow for the flavor of the spirit.

Ingredients

- 1 cup honey
- 1/2 cup water
- zest of 1/2 an orange, no white pith
- 1 stick cinnamon (optional)
- 1 1/2 cups vodka

Directions

- Heat the honey, water, orange zest, and cinnamon over medium heat, stirring frequently until it makes a syrup, about 10 - 12 minutes. Remove any foam and let cool.
- Once cooled, remove the zest and cinnamon.
- Then combine the honey syrup and alcohol in a sealable glass jar, seal, and shake.
- For best flavor, allow to rest for a couple days.
- Bottle (no need for refrigeration).

Irish Cream (Bailey's clone)

Bailey's Irish Cream, among others, is a very popular cream liqueur that can be fairly successfully replicated. The one thing we won't be able to replicate is their special process that allows 2 year, unrefrigerated shelf life, so we will be refrigerating our product, since it does contain milk products. I include a couple different recipe versions. Pick the one you like!

Ingredients

- 1 1/2 cups evaporated milk (12 ounce can)
- 1 cup whiskey or moonshine (Irish whiskey is best)
- 2/3 cup simple syrup or white sugar
- 1 tablespoon chocolate syrup
- 1 teaspoon vanilla extract
- 3/4 teaspoon instant coffee

Directions

- combine all ingredients in a blender, cover securely and mix well until sugar is dissolved and everything amalgamates.
- refrigerate and shake before serving.

Irish Cream 2

This is also very tasty! You may have trouble picking the one you like!

Ingredients

- 1 can (375-400 ml) sweetened condensed milk (Eagle brand for eg)
- same amount of cream (18-35 percent depending how rich you want it)
- same amount of vodka, moonshine or Irish Whiskey (use the can to measure)
- 4 tablespoons chocolate syrup (Hershey's etc.)
- 1 teaspoon vanilla extract
- 1 teaspoon coconut extract
- 2 teaspoons instant coffee

Directions

- Use a blender or container large enough for all ingredients
- Put all ingredients in blender, in above order
- Blend on high for at least 30 seconds until ingredients are incorporated
- Bottle and refrigerate
- Shake before serving

Jägermeister

Jägermeister is a German liqueur, literally translated meaning 'Hunting-master'. According to their website, 56 herbs, fruits, roots and spices are used in its making. Dating from 1878, it was originally used as a *digestif*, now popular as a liqueur. Of course, the recipe is a closely guarded secret, but I've included a starting point for you to get pretty close to the taste.

Ingredients

- 1 1/2 litres moonshine or vodka
- 4 ounces of black liquorice
- one inch piece of ginger root, peeled
- 3 inch piece of cinnamon stick
- 2 teaspoons star anise seeds
- 1/2 teaspoon cardamom seeds
- 1/2 teaspoon fennel seeds
- peel or zest of 1/2 bitter orange (no white pith)
- peel or zest of 1/2 sweet orange (no pith)
- 2 allspice berries
- small sprig of fresh thyme (or 1/4 teaspoon dry)
- 1/4 teaspoon black pepper
- 1/4 teaspoon nutmeg
- 1/4 teaspoon coriander
- pinch of lavender flowers
- pinch of saffron
- pinch of camomile
- 1 tablespoon clover honey
- 5 tablespoons liquid sweet caramel

Directions

- Chop liquorice and put in blender with half the alcohol. Blend well.
- Put in large enough aging container to hold all ingredients

- Crush all herbs and spices (not orange peel, honey or caramel)
- Add remainder of alcohol with crushed herbs, spices and orange peel
- Shake daily for 2 to 4 days, tasting daily until satisfied with flavour
- Filter ingredients out with coffee filter(s)
- Add clover honey and caramel and mix well
- Allow to settle out, siphon and bottle cleared liquor

Bear in mind, the original Jägermeister is aged in oak for a year or more, which contributes to its dark colour. That's partly why I used black liquorice at the beginning, to help impart the darker colour (along with the caramel). Aging this will also help amalgamate the flavours.

If you have difficulty finding lavender flowers, saffron or camomile, these may be omitted.

Other possible spices you can add include orris root, galengal, lovage, chiretta, angelica, hyssop, pomerance, cloves, rose hips, tumeric, mace, yarrow, burdock, wintergreen, juniper berries, ginseng, borage and sandalwood. These would be in very small quantities compared to the rest of the 'major' ingredients.

Jägermeister is bottled at 35% ABV. You should be close to this, but if you want to be totally true to the original, add a little water to bring it to 35% (70 proof). Aging will definitely improve this, helping amalgamate flavours and giving it a little more smoothness.

One myth surrounding this liquor is that it contains deer blood. It does not, so don't even go there.

Have fun with the recipe, and feel free to put your own spin on it! I include an online source of herbs in the appendix.

Kűmmel

Kűmmel is an Old World liqueur...some would argue German, some Russian...but it is caraway based, often used as an aperitif before or after dinner. Because of its savoury nature, you could also use it in cooking meat or vegetable dishes.

Ingredients

- 3 tablespoons caraway seeds
- 1/4 teaspoon fennel seeds
- 2 whole cloves
- 1 litre vodka or moonshine
- 1 cup white sugar
- 1/2 cup water

Directions

- Crack or bruise caraway and fennel seeds with a pestle or wooden spoon
- Put in sealable container with cloves and add alcohol
- Shake well and age 1 day
- After 1 day, remove cloves and continue to age for 2 weeks
- Strain seeds out of liquor
- Heat water and dissolve sugar
- Cool and add to strained liquor, tasting as you go. Some may like this less sweet to preserve a more savoury flavour.

Limoncello

An interesting story how I came upon this recipe. My sister was in Italy on holiday, and toured a distillery which manufactured Limoncello. Knowing that I liked Limoncello and Crema Limoncello, she (maybe naively) asked the owner for the recipes. Unbelievably, the owner took the pages out of her notebook, photocopied them and handed them to my sister. I was shocked and amazed, but very grateful to have the authentic recipes!

Ingredients

- 10 average size lemons (if large, use 7 or 8)
- 1 litre alcohol (vodka or moonshine) 75-80% alcohol (150-160 proof)
- 1/2 litre lemon juice
- 1 1/2 kilograms white sugar
- 1 litre water

Directions

- Zest the lemons (no white pith), and place into a large glass bottle or jar.
- Pour in alcohol. Cover well and let infuse for one week at room temperature, shaking or stirring each day.
- After one week, combine sugar, lemon juice and water in a medium saucepan. Bring to a low boil. Boil for 15 minutes, *not* stirring.
- Allow syrup to cool to room temperature (important!).
- Strain zest from alcohol and stir alcohol into syrup.
- Let mixture settle for a few days, and siphon off cleared liqueur
- Bottle and seal. Age for 2 weeks.
- To serve, put bottled liqueur in the freezer. When icy cold, serve in chilled vodka glasses or shot glasses.

Crema Limoncello

The other version of the Italian distillery's recipe…this one is my favourite!

Ingredients

- 10 medium lemons (8 or 9 large)
- 1 1/2 litres alcohol (grain or moonshine) 75-80% ABV (150 - 160 proof)
- 2 vanilla beans
- 2 litres skim milk
- 2 kilograms white sugar

Directions

- Zest the lemons (no white pith) and place in glass sealable jar.
- Add the alcohol and let stand at room temperature for 10-14 days, shaking or stirring daily.
- After steeping, heat milk to a low boil and add sugar and vanilla beans.
- Simmer for 15 minutes on medium heat. Remove any scum.
- Let milk mixture cool and remove vanilla beans.
- Strain off the lemon peels/zest from the alcohol and stir alcohol into cooled milk mixture.
- Bottle and keep refrigerated.

Note that lemon juice is not used in this recipe. I do juice them so as not to waste them, but refrigerate it for lemonade or other uses. Recipe may be halved if desired.

Key Lime Liqueur

This is a lovely, refreshing summery liqueur. Use it in baking or cooking also!

Ingredients

- 6 key limes (or regular limes)

- 1 cup light rum

- 1 cup vodka or moonshine

- 2 cups sugar

Directions

- Zest the limes and juice them; do not use white pith, which is bitter

- Add all ingredients into a sealable container

- Steep for 3 - 4 weeks

- Shake or stir every day for a week, then twice a week thereafter

- Strain out fruit and peel, and filter through coffee filter(s) if needed

- Dilute with water a bit if you wish a lower alcohol level

- Bottle

Mango Liqueur

If you like mangos, you'll appreciate this fresh, fruity liqueur! Again, best to use ripe fruit…unripe fruit won't give you as much flavour or aroma.

Ingredients

- 4 large mangos, peeled, pitted and chopped
- 1/4 cup lemon juice
- zest or peel from 1/2 of a lemon (no white pith)
- 2 1/2 cups white sugar
- 2 cups vodka or moonshine
- 1 cup light rum

Directions

- Peel and pit mangos and chop into small pieces
- combine all ingredients into a sealable container and mix well until sugar is dissolved.
- Age in refrigerator or a cool dark place for 3-4 weeks, shaking regularly
- Strain out fruit and press lightly to get juice and alcohol out
- Allow to sit a few days until liquor clears
- Siphon or pour off cleared liqueur carefully and discard settlings (or use on ice cream!)
- Bottle

Maple Liqueur

This one is as easy as it gets...great flavour too! I've found that a dark maple syrup is more flavourful, so I would recommend using that.

Ingredients

- 2 cups rye whiskey, vodka or moonshine
- 2 cups real maple syrup

Directions

- Pour the alcohol into a sealable glass jar or bottle
- Stir in the maple syrup until dissolved
- Store in the refrigerator

For more complexity, add a vanilla bean and age for a couple days with the bean in the bottle. Remove and discard vanilla bean or put it in a container with some sugar. (The sugar will absorb the vanilla flavour over time, and you can use this infused sugar when you need vanilla in other recipes!)

Melon Liqueur

This can make a very tasty liqueur, depending on the melon you use. A fragrant, robust melon will greatly improve your final product. Also, use a ripe melon. Green or unripe melons won't be nearly as flavourful. I recommend honeydew, cantaloupe or a tigger melon if you can find it!

Ingredients

- 4 cups chopped melon (no rind) - remove seeds
- 2 cups vodka
- 2 cups white sugar

Directions

- Puree melon in a blender or food processor or mash well to release juice and break down flesh
- Mix in sugar until dissolved
- Place melon in a large enough sealable container and add alcohol
- Refrigerate and let age for at least 3 weeks
- Shake or stir at least once a day for the first week, and twice a week thereafter.
- Strain solids out of liqueur, pressing gently to get the most juice possible
- Let sit for a few days undisturbed in frig to allow settling
- Siphon off cleared liqueur or pour carefully
- If necessary, strain through coffee filter(s)
- Bottle and refrigerate

Mint Liqueur

Similar to Crème de Menthe, but this recipe uses fresh mint leaves to provide a mild, fresh liqueur that you may like even better.

Ingredients

- 2 cups fresh mint leaves, lightly packed
- 1 litre vodka or moonshine (80 proof ~ 40 ABV)
- 2 1/2 cups white sugar
- 1 1/2 cups water
- 1 teaspoon glycerine (optional)
- 10 drops green food colouring (optional)
- 3 drops blue food colouring (optional)

Directions

- Wash mint leaves well with plain water and let dry
- Chop into smaller pieces, discarding stems
- Put into sealable container
- Boil water and dissolve sugar
- Cool sugar solution and add to chopped mint leaves
- Add alcohol and steep for 2 - 3 weeks
- Strain out leaves and filter through coffee filter(s) if necessary
- If desired, stir in glycerine and food colouring (a few drops at a time)
- Bottle and age at least a month

Ouzo

This is a Greek liquor that they proudly like to drink in straight shots!
Anise or liquorice flavoured, it's more of a liquor than a liqueur. It is usually flavoured, then distilled, like other liquors. Here's a starting point for you.

Ingredients

- 1 litre vodka or moonshine 40% (80 proof)
- 1 1/2 ounces (45g) anise seed
- 2/3 ounce (20g) fennel seed
- 1/3 ounce (10g) star anise
- 1/6 ounce (5g) dried angelica root
- 1/2 cup simple syrup (optional)
- other optional herbs you can use include pinches of cinnamon, clove, coriander, linden blossom, cardamom, and mint.

Directions

- Crush herbs, add to alcohol, close in a sealable food grade container.
- Shake well to combine
- Macerate at room temperature for 5 to 7 days
- Strain/filter off herbs and allow liquor to clear.
- Siphon or carefully pour off cleared liquor.
- Bottle

Alternate methods:

Instead of macerating the moonshine with the herbs, you can add the herbs to the primary fermenting wash. The problem with this method is that it will take much more herb volume since much of it will stay with the water when it is distilled off. This will save time however in macerating and clearing. You should use probably 4 to 5 times as much.

Another method, especially if a pure, clean colour is desired, is to macerate then re-distill the alcohol, much the same as making Absinthe. A small secondary maceration may be required, or simply add a bit more herb mixture to the primary maceration.

Pastis

Pastis was developed out of a need for a liqueur similar to absinthe, after that was banned in France, among other countries. Also a liquorice-flavoured liquor, Pastis is traditionally lower in alcohol than Absinthe, which was often served at 140 proof! Unlike Absinthe, it is made without wormwood, which is the herb that was blamed on Absinthe's alleged hallucinogenic properties! While Anisette is primarily flavoured with aniseed, Pastis is mostly flavoured with star anise. Use Chinese star anise, as Japanese is poisonous!

Ingredients

- 1 litre moonshine, vodka or plain grain alcohol 40-45% (80-90 proof)
- 15 - 20 whole star anise pods depending on size
- 2 tablespoons ground or finely chopped licorice root
- 1 teaspoon anise seeds
- 1 teaspoon fennel seeds
- 1/2 teaspoon coriander seeds
- 2/3 cup simple syrup (or to taste)

Directions

- Crush or grind herbs
- Mix well with alcohol and seal in food grade container.
- Macerate for about 7 to 10 days in a cool dark place, shake occasionally.
- Strain or filter out herbs and let stand until clear
- Siphon off cleared liquor.
- Add simple syrup and mix well.
- Bottle and age for a few days.

As with Absinthe, Pastis is often served with cold water, diluting it with 1 or 2 times the volume of water.

Notes: This recipe will benefit by the addition of a few drops of anise oil, which will help the drink 'louche', or turn white when water is added (as it is sometimes served). Anise oil can be fairly expensive, but if you choose to add it, you can cut down a little on anise seeds or star anise. Add it at the beginning of the steep to ensure it is well mixed in.

Peach Liqueur (similar to Southern Comfort)

This liqueur will remind you of summer whenever you take a sip! Lovely fresh fruit taste and bouquet to tease your senses! Although it's whiskey based, you can make it with unflavoured spirit also.

Ingredients

- 2 pounds peaches
- 1 1/4 cups white sugar
- 1/2 cup water
- Peel or zest half of a small lemon
- Peel or zest half of an orange
- 2 1/2 cups vodka, moonshine or best...bourbon

Directions

- Peel and pit the peaches, chopping into small chunks
- Zest or peel half a small lemon and half an orange
- Place in a pot over low heat; add water and sugar, stirring well to dissolve sugar. The heat will help get juice out of the peaches. Don't boil though.
- Cool and put in sealable aging container. Add peels and alcohol
- Refrigerate and age for 7 to 10 days
- Sieve fruit from liqueur and remove peel, pressing the peaches gently to get the juice and alcohol out
- (you can use the peach pulp in other recipes such as jam or jelly!)
- Let strained liqueur sit undisturbed for a few days until it clears
- If necessary, strain through coffee filter(s)
- Bottle

Pear Liqueur

This is a lovely, light liqueur that will be sure to please! Be sure to use nice ripe pears, wash the fruit well, but leave skins in if you want added colour.

Ingredients:

- 5 or 6 large pears ~ 6 or 7 smaller ones
- 2 1/4 cups white sugar
- 4 cups (1 litre) vodka or moonshine (or 2 cups vodka, 2 cups brandy)
- 1 teaspoon glycerine (optional)

Directions

- Wash pears, trim tops and bottoms, remove seeds
- Chop into chunks and place in sealable container
- Add sugar and alcohol and shake until mixed well
- Age for 6 weeks in refrigerator or cool dark place, stirring or shaking regularly
- Strain out fruit and press lightly to get juice/alcohol out
- Discard the fruit, or use it to make 'drunk pear jam'!!
- Let stand a few days until liqueur clears, then siphon or pour off cleared liqueur
- If need be, strain through coffee filter(s)
- Stir in glycerine if desired
- Bottle

Peppermint Liqueur

Some people may call this peppermint schnapps, although a true schnapps wouldn't be as sweet. Reduce the sugar if desired.

Ingredients

- 3/4 cup white sugar
- 1 1/4 cups light corn syrup
- 2 cups vodka
- 2 teaspoons peppermint extract

Directions

- In a pot, heat corn syrup over a medium heat. Dissolve sugar, stirring regularly, about 5 or 10 minutes
- Remove from heat and cool
- Stir in vodka and peppermint extract.
- Bottle

Pina Colada Liqueur

This is a very summery drink, usually served as a cocktail made with pineapple, coconut milk and rum. As a liqueur, we are using flaked coconut instead of milk.

Ingredients

- 2 cups flaked sweetened coconut
- 1 1/2 cups white sugar
- 1 1/2 cups water
- 1/2 of a vanilla bean, split open
- 2 cups fresh or canned unsweetened pineapple
- 3 cups light or amber rum

Directions

- Bring water to a low boil and add white sugar, stirring to dissolve
- Reduce heat to low and add coconut and vanilla bean
- Simmer for 10 minutes, stirring often
- Remove from heat and cool, remove vanilla bean
- Crush and add pineapple and stir into mixture
- Place in sealable container, and when room temperature, add alcohol
- Refrigerate and age for 4-5 weeks, shaking at least twice weekly
- Strain and allow liqueur to stand a few days to clear
- When cleared, siphon or carefully pour cleared liquid from sediment
- Filter through coffee filter(s) if necessary
- Bottle

Pineapple Liqueur

This is a very simple but tasty liqueur you can either enjoy by itself, or mix with other liquors or juices. Traditionally called **Stoli Doli**, it is served like a martini, shaken with ice! Many bars use large, clear jars to show off this liquor with carefully arranged chunks or rings of pineapple as it steeps.

Ingredients

- 1 fresh sweet pineapple, at least 2-3 pounds (1 kilogram+)
- 3 cups (750 ml) moonshine or vodka

Directions

- Cut outer rind off of pineapple and discard
- Chop into pieces and put into sealable container
- Add alcohol
- Steep for 7 to 10 days at room temperature
- Strain off alcohol and lightly press pineapple to get remainder of juice and alcohol
- Filter through coffee filter(s) if needed, or allow to clear, then siphon cleared juice off
- Store in refrigerator

Note: If needed, canned pineapple can be used, although fresh is better. If added sweetness is desired, a little simple syrup may be added after steeping.

Plum Liqueur

This is a lovely, fruity liqueur that some may relate to the European liquor Slivovitz. However, Slivovitz is distilled from the fermented fruit with no sugar added. I have a separate recipe for this if you wish to make it the traditional way.

Ingredients

- 2 1/2 pounds of sweet plums
- 2 1/2 cups white sugar
- 2 cups moonshine or vodka
- 1 cup brandy

Directions

- Mash the plums with the sugar, incorporating sugar well into fruit (leave skins on for colour, pit if desired)
- Put in a sealable container
- Add alcohols, mix well and seal
- Refrigerate or place in a cool dark place for at least 6 weeks, shaking or stirring regularly
- Strain out plum pulp, pressing well to get juice and alcohol out
- Allow liqueur to stand for a few days until liquor clears
- Siphon or pour alcohol off of settlings carefully
- Filter with coffee filter(s) if necessary
- Bottle

Raspberry (or fruit) Liqueur

For something simpler to make than Chambord, but still with great raspberry flavour, this is much easier!

Ingredients

- 3/4 litre of vodka or moonshine (about 3 cups)
- 2 cups sugar
- 3 cups raspberries

Directions

- Crush berries and add sugar, mixing until dissolved
- Put in a sealable glass or food grade container and add alcohol
- Seal and refrigerate for at least 8 weeks.
- Strain solids out of liquor, pressing berries gently to get juice and alcohol out.

You can substitute many fruits using this formula. Citrus fruits may vary from this a bit, because generally the zest or peel is used, rather than the pulp or juice of citrus fruits, but berries will be much the same as this recipe. You can even combine fruits that you like, such as a field berry medley of blueberry, strawberry and raspberry for instance. Just keep the combined total to the above amounts. If using strong flavoured fruit, lemon for example, you can use a bit less fruit in maceration, milder flavours such as melon may require a bit more.

Rhubarb Liqueur

Rhubarb is an old time favourite, often used for pies or cakes. Not particularly sweet and quite acidic, it has a very distinctive taste and aroma that will remind you of your grandmother's baking!

Ingredients

- 4 cups fresh, ripe rhubarb (try to use reddish colour fruit for best colour)
- 3 cups white sugar
- 3 cups moonshine or vodka

Directions

- Dice rhubarb into small pieces, or use food processor to mince it up
- Stir in sugar and dissolve as much as possible
- Place in a sealable container and add alcohol
- Place in a cool dark place for 3 to 4 weeks, shaking or stirring regularly
- Strain out fruit and press to get juice (discard rhubarb or use it for jam)
- Allow to settle and clear a couple days, then pour or siphon off cleared liqueur
- Filter if necessary through coffee filter(s)
- Bottle

If you want to add a bit more complexity, add a handful of fresh strawberries, which are often used with rhubarb in baking.

Rice Whiskey

As with most liquors, there are many variations of rice beverages, some are wine based, some liquors. This recipe will give you a basic rice whiskey recipe, which you can alter by using different varieties of rice, such as sweet rice, jasmine rice, or simply plain white rice for a neutral liquor (like lao-lao in Laos). Because it is a grain, therefore starch based, you will need the addition of an enzyme such as amylase to convert starches into fermentable sugars.

Ingredients

- 5 gallons water
- 4 kilograms rice (I suggest sweet rice for it's higher starch/sugar content) (others, such as long grain brown rice are lower in starch so use a little more)
- 3 tablespoons lemon juice
- 1 1/2 teaspoons amylase enzyme
- package of whiskey yeast, or whatever alcohol yeast you want to use

Directions

- cook the rice in water (if you can't do entire amount at once, do it in batches - it will swell and thicken a lot, and you don't want it to burn).
- when well cooked, add it to fermenting container and top up with hot water to about 150 degrees F. (amylase enzyme works best about that temp).
- (you could use malted grain to act as the enzyme, but it wouldn't be a 100 percent rice alcohol then)

- add enzyme, stir well and allow to sit for several hours. You will note the thickness will lessen as the starches are converted into sugars.
- add lemon juice and stir in.
- make sure temperature is below 90 degrees F., and add yeast.
- cover and allow to ferment to dryness.
- strain out rice and fill still with wash.
- distill in a pot still (or reflux for neutral spirit) (heads will be minimal).

As a rule, short grain white rice has more starch content than long grain rice varieties. Scented rices such as Jasmine or Basmati can add a nice bouquet to your liquor if you choose to pot distill.

Rumtopf

This recipe can be a lot of fun, and a showcase for your entertaining! A German word literally meaning *'rum pot'*, Rumtopf celebrates fruit coming into season, and preserved in alcohol for Christmas or other winter holiday. Basically, you add a different fruit to the pot containing rum as each comes into season. Most fruit can be used, although not usually citrus.

Ingredients

Start with the earliest berries in season, usually strawberries. You can use whatever fruit appeals to you, about 3 cups of each (roughly a pound). I list some example fruits below. By the time you're done, you should have 5 or 6 different kinds of fruit, combined with sugar and rum.

- 1 cup white sugar for each fruit added
- 1 litre of light or amber rum
- 3 cups ripe strawberries, washed and stemmed. Do not mash them. Either use small berries whole (recommended), or big berries cut in half.
- 3 cups ripe whole raspberries, loganberries or blackberries
- 3 cups pitted ripe cherries, any kind (sweeter are better)
- 3 cups blueberries
- 3 cups peaches, peeled and sliced

Directions

- You will need a very large glass jar or crock. There are actually containers specifically made for this! Search the internet!
- Sterilize container well since this will take several months to make
- Put the strawberries in container and add 1 cup of sugar, mixing gently.
- Let stand for half an hour then pour in rum. No need to stir.
- Cover and keep in refrigerator for the duration of aging
- You should allow 2-3 weeks between additions if possible
- For each additional fruit, mix in a bowl with a cup of sugar and let stand for 1/2 hour before adding to container
- Repeat for each subsequent fruit as they come into season.
- You should end up with 5 or 6 fruits, which will be wonderfully steeped in alcohol, and looking great. This is used as is, no pressing or straining!
- Serve at your Holiday dinner spooned over white cake, or ice cream, then get ready for the rave reviews, especially because you did it yourself!

Slivovitz

Slivovitz is very much an ethnic liquor, most popular in eastern and central Europe, particularly Slavic countries such as Serbia, Slovenia, Croatia, Bosnia, Czech Republic, Slovakia, Poland, Hungary, and Bulgaria. Made from Damson or 'sugar plum', it is traditionally made without sugar, and distilled to a fairly high alcohol content, about 100 proof. Other countries may call it plum brandy, and may have a bit lower ABV, about 80 proof.

To make traditional Slivovitz, it will take at least 10 kg of plums to end up with about a litre of liquor. Use only the most ripe fruit, since you are relying on the sugar content of the fruit alone. The sweeter they are the fewer you need!

Crush or mash it well (can leave skins on and stones in if you want) and add a wine yeast (old timers simply rely on wild yeast to ferment, but if you've read this far, you'll know that I recommend a good wine yeast). You will also need a little yeast nutrient.

Cover and let ferment to dryness (fermentation will stop and mash will no longer taste sweet). This will probably take at least 2 -3 weeks.

Strain out plums and press well to get all the juice and alcohol out. (Again, old timers would just distill the entire mash, but that can be a real mess cleaning the still, and you risk burning the fruit, giving it an off taste)

Distil the fermented juice in a pot still, slowly, so as to retain the most fragrance of the fruit. Again, traditionally, this is double distilled. If you are using a good quality modern still, this may not be necessary.

Check proof with an alcoholmeter and decide how strong you want it, and if necessary, dilute with distilled water. If not strong enough, re-distil

For another recipe using plums...but less traditional...see Plum Liqueur.

Spiced Brandy

This is a lovely holiday treat for you and your guests. It can be served warm or cold (don't heat too much though, or you'll evaporate the alcohol!). You can also mix it with another favourite liqueur to give add a spicy flavour!

Ingredients

Use your favourite spice flavours, fresh are better than ground. Example, allspice, cloves, cinnamon sticks, ginger root, or nutmeg.

- 4 tablespoons of your chosen spices, crushed or coarsely chopped
- 3 juniper berries
- Zest or peel of 1 tangerine or orange (no white pith)
- Juice of tangerine or orange
- 3 cups brandy (moonshine or vodka can be used instead, but increase amount of brown sugar and reduce white in proportion)
- 1 cup brown sugar
- 3/4 cup white sugar
- 1 cup water

Directions

- Heat water and dissolve sugars
- Remove from heat and add spices, juice and peel
- Put in sealable container
- Allow to cool and add alcohol
- Let steep for 2 - 3 weeks
- Stir daily and taste. Some flavours can become overpowering, such as nutmeg, cloves and allspice.
- When happy with the flavour, strain out spices and peel
- Let the alcohol settle until clear, then bottle cleared liquor

As a variation, use rum instead of brandy, and add it to regular rum to make a nice spiced rum. Any rum will do, from light to dark!

Spiced Rum

Making your own spiced rum can be a fun and rewarding experience, especially at seasonal get-togethers! Suggested spices are included, but if you have other favorites, go ahead and make it your own!

Ingredients

1 - liter of your preferred rum (see rum recipe above, or commercial)
1 - vanilla bean, split lengthwise
1 - cinnamon stick, crushed or chopped
4 - whole allspice berries
5 - whole black peppercorns
1 - whole nutmeg berry or a pinch of grated nutmeg
2 - 2-inch pieces of fresh ginger
3 - 3-inch strips orange zest

Directions

- Mix your favorite ingredients as suggested above with 1 liter of rum
- Seal in container and age from 5-10 days depending on your desired taste and strength
- Strain out spices and filter through coffee filters if necessary
- Bottle and enjoy!

Other possible spices could include an anise or star anise seed if you like a licorice flavor, another type of zest instead of or in addition to orange, or simply a bit more or less of the ones suggested above, according to your liking.

Strawberry Liqueur

Very similar to raspberry liqueur, this is best made with fresh, in season fruit (as is the case for most fruit liqueurs!). This style recipe is easy and can be applied to other fruit simply by changing the berries you use!

Ingredients

- 3/4 litre of vodka or moonshine (about 3 cups)
- 1 1/2 - 2 cups sugar (more if you like sweeter, less if you don't)
- 3 cups ripe strawberries

Directions

- Crush berries and add sugar, mixing until dissolved
- Put in a sealable glass or food grade container and add alcohol
- Seal and refrigerate for at least 8 weeks.
- Strain solids out of liquor, pressing berries gently to get the most juice and alcohol out.
- If need be, filter through coffee (filters)
- Bottle

You can substitute many fruits (especially berries) using this formula. Citrus fruits may vary from this a bit, because generally the zest or peel is used, rather than the pulp or juice of citrus fruits, but berries will be much the same as this recipe. You can even combine fruits that you like, such as a field berry medley of blueberry, strawberry and raspberry for instance. Just keep the combined fruit total to the above amounts.

Tea Liqueur

Although certainly not everyone's cup of tea (pun intended!), if you are a tea lover, you can certainly make a very nice liqueur from your favourite tea.

Ingredients

The ingredients for this will vary a bit with personal taste, but the basic recipe follows. You can use more or less sweetener, according to what you like. If you like, you can add additional ingredients such as a couple pieces of orange peel for some extra flavour complexity.

- 2 tablespoons tea leaves (whatever your flavour preference)
- 1 cup hot (not boiling) water
- 1/2 litre moonshine or vodka
- 1/2 cup simple syrup or light honey

Directions

- Steep tea leaves in hot water until cool.
- add alcohol and steep for another 12 hours (no longer…tannins in the tea leaves will make your liqueur bitter)
- Strain out tea leaves
- Sweeten to taste with simple syrup or honey
- Let mature for a few days

Triple Sec

There is a lot of confusion over the term 'triple sec'. Some people think it means triple distilled, some that 3 different types of oranges are used in it's making, some think of it as a generic term for orange liqueur. In this recipe, I'm going to opt for using a triple orange method, in case your friends ask 'what is triple sec?', you have an easy explanation.

Ingredients

- 8 medium size naval or other sweet oranges
- 1 bitter orange or a tablespoon of dried bitter orange peel
- 1 tablespoon orange flower water
- 4 cups white sugar
- 1 cup water
- 1 1/4 cups orange juice (from sweet oranges)
- 1 litre 80 proof (40%) vodka or moonshine

Directions

- Peel all oranges (zest only, no white pith) and put in a sealable container
- Juice the sweet oranges, but not the bitter one
- Using the water and orange juice, make a simple syrup with sugar
- Heat but do not boil the simple syrup until sugar dissolves
- Add hot syrup to orange peels
- Stir and let cool
- Add orange flower water and vodka
- Stir and seal and place in cool dark place
- Age in a cool dark place for 30 days, shaking regularly
- Strain and let mixture settle out.
- Bottle and enjoy

This will make about 2 - 750 litre bottles of about 30% alcohol (there may be a bit left over for you to taste test ☺!). You can adjust sweetness up or down depending on your desire.

Vermouth

Technically a fortified wine, usually around 20% alcohol by volume, you can make your own vermouth using moonshine or vodka. You need to either make your own wine first, or buy a white wine you like, and proceed from there.

Ingredients

- 1 litre white wine
- 100 - 200 g sugar
- 1 cup (250 ml) moonshine or vodka
- 1 stick cinnamon
- 1 clove
- pinch of oregano
- pinch of sweet basil
- pinch of wormwood
- pinch of sage
- pinch of coriander
- pinch of gentian root
- zest or peel from 1 large orange (no white pith)

Directions

- In a sealable container, add wine, moonshine, sugar, cinnamon, sage sweet basil, oregano and coriander and mix well
- Seal and steep for 4 days in a cool dark place.
- Add wormwood, clove and gentian root
- Steep for one or two more days
- Strain through coffee filters, let clear and bottle
- Aging for a week will help flavour mature

The reason for the split addition of ingredients is because the wormwood and gentian provide bitterness, which can become overpowering if allowed to steep too long, as can the clove. The other herbs and spices provide most of the flavor. You can adjust the sugar content up or down, depending how sweet you like it.

Appendix

The following sources are for reference and your convenience. I have not used all of these sources, but compiled them here for your information. It is by no means a complete resource...there are undoubtedly many many more small stores and suppliers. I merely compiled a list of some of the larger, better known sources.

And, I take no responsibility for what you order or how you use it. As I've stated throughout this book, research, understand and make sure you know what you're doing before you do it!

Links to still designs :

(In their designs, they use water tanks. Be sure what you use are copper or stainless steel interiors)

2 inch column design
http://journeytoforever.org/biofuel_library/ethanol_motherearth/meCh9a.html

3 inch column design
http://journeytoforever.org/biofuel_library/ethanol_motherearth/meCh8.html - 8-2

4 inch column design
http://journeytoforever.org/biofuel_library/ethanol_motherearth/meCh9b.html

Instructional Videos

Still assembly videos by Clawhammer Supply show how to assemble their own stills. As well as giving you a good idea of whether or not you have the skills necessary to build a still, these videos provide a good basic understanding of how to build and assemble a still, using basic tools:
http://www.clawhammersupply.com/pages/moonshine-videos

Rainier Distillery has uploaded a lot of YouTube videos on everything from alcohol distillation to essential oil extraction.
http://www.youtube.com/playlist?list=UU4TJceC6wVGErnoWblqafAw

Hillbilly Stills has a number of videos on their website, mostly to do with their equipment, but still a valuable learning experience to see professional set-up and how it works.
http://www.hillbillystills.com/moonshine_still_videos_s/86.htm

Equipment and Ingredient Suppliers

United States:

http://www.moonshinestuff.com/
An Amazon store with one of the widest selections of everything I've seen!

http://moonshinedistiller.com/
Variety of equipment, supplies and ingredients
Fraser, Colorado

http://www.brewhaus.com/
Wide variety of equipment, supplies and ingredients
Keller, Texas

http://www.hillbillystills.com/
Wide variety of equipment & supplies
Kentucky

https://distillery-equipment.com/
Large stills, mash and fermenting vessels (30 gal. +)
Doniphan, MO

http://www.milehidistilling.com/
Wide variety of equipment & supplies
Lakewood, Colorado

http://www.coppermoonshinestills.com/
All-copper still manufacturer
Fort Smith, Arizona

http://shop.rainierdistillers.com/
Wide variety of hardware & equipment
Yelm, Washington

http://www.clawhammersupply.com/
Three different stills kits offered, but assembly is required (and therefore tools and skills)!!
Fort Collins, Colorado

http://www.norcalbrewingsolutions.com/
Brewing & distilling supplies & equipment
Redding, California

http://www.moonshinestillpro.com/
Stills, parts and accessories
St. Louis, Missouri

http://www.moonshinestill.com/
Small assortment of copper stills
no location given

http://www.whiskeystill.net/
Small assortment of copper stills
Houston, Texas

http://www.homebrewheaven.com/
Brewing supplies, grains, some distilling supplies
Everett, WA

http://arcticbrewingsupply.com/
Brewing supplies, grains, no stills
Anchorage, Alaska
*ships only within Alaska

For Herbs and spices
http://www.iherb.com/?rcode=DTH933
(This link will also get you a discount on your first order!)

Also: Mountain Rose Herbs
http://www.mountainroseherbs.com/

Canada:

http://www.moonshinestuff.com/
An Amazon store with one of the widest selections of everything I've seen!

www.homebrewsupplies.ca
Grains, malts, brewing equipment., extracts, some equipment
Brampton, Ontario

www.brewhaus.ca
Good selection of extracts, yeasts some stills & equipment.
Brewhaus Canada

www.home-distilling.com
Wide choice of essences, yeasts, stills, equipment & supplies
Nepean, Ontario

www.beergrains.com
Good selection of grains, malts, brewing equipment, *no stills
Deep River, Ontario

http://www.brewersdirect.com/
Brewing and distilling supplies   Winnipeg, Manitoba

http://www.homecraft.on.ca/distilling
Small selection of stills, supplies   Kingston, Ontario

http://brokenoardistillingequipment.com/
Small supplier of various sized stills   Nanaimo, British Columbia

http://www.torontobrewing.ca/
Brewing supplies, grains, no stills   Toronto, Ontario

For Herbs and spices

http://www.iherb.com/?rcode=DTH933
(This link will also get you a discount on your first order!)

United Kingdom

http://www.moonshinestuff.com/
An Amazon store with one of the widest selections of everything I've seen!

http://www.homebrewmegastore.co.uk/
Stills, filters, pumps, wide variety of supplies
Brownhills, West Midlands, UK

http://www.lovebrewing.co.uk/
Couple of stills, variety of supplies
Chesterfield & Liverpool, UK

http://www.the-home-brew-shop.co.uk/
Couple of stills, some supplies
Aldershot, Hapshire, UK

http://www.brew2bottle.co.uk/
Couple of stills, some supplies
Northwich, Cheshire

http://www.brewingsupplies.co.uk/
Couple of stills, some supplies
Nottingham, UK

http://www.brewstore.co.uk/
Couple of stills, some supplies, grains, equipment
Edinburgh, UK

http://www.goodlifehomebrew.com/
Good selection of stills, supplies and equipment
Norwich, Norfolk, UK

http://www.thehomebrewboat.co.uk/
Couple of stills, some supplies
mobile boat travelling UK canals

http://www.discountbrew.co.uk/
Couple of stills, some supplies   Hapton, Norfolk, UK

http://www.homebrewcentregy.com/
Couple stills, good selection of supplies
Grimsby, UK

Australia

http://shop.beerbelly.com.au/
Mostly brewing supplies, but also fermenting equipment and grains
Adelaide, SA

http://www.stilldragon.com.au/
Stills, equipment and parts
Tamworth NSW

http://www.brewcraftsa.com.au/
Smaller stills, equipment and supplies (brewing & wine also).
Torrensville, SA

http://www.ibrew.com.au/
Stills 30 l. and less, equipment and supplies (brewing & wine also).
Parkwood, QLD

New Zealand

http://www.spiritsandbrewing.co.nz/
A few stills, good selection of supplies

http://yourshout.co.nz/index.html
Stills, brewing, distilling supplies
Christchurch

For Herbs and spices

http://www.iherb.com/?rcode=DTH933
(This link will also get you a discount on your first order!)

Other International

https://www.destillatio.eu/en/
Large selection of stills and equipment and ingredients
Buchenau, Germany

http://www.turbogist.nl/
Brewing supplies, some equipment, no stills
Leende, Netherlands

http://www.copper-alembic.com/ns/
Good selection of copper stills, equipment, some ingredients
Valenca, Portugal

http://www.brouwland.com/en/
Wide selection of equipment and supplies
Belgium

http://partymanshop.com/en/
*Supplies, some equipment *no stills*
Svedala, Sweden

http://distillique.co.za/distilling_shop/
Stills, supplies, good variety of everything
Gauteng, South Africa

http://www.doctorguber.ru/en/alcohol/catalog/stuff/
Stills and equipment
St. Petersburg, Moscow, Russia

For Herbs and spices

http://www.iherb.com/?rcode=DTH933
(This link will also get you a discount on your first order!)

Notes

Printed in Great Britain
by Amazon

21156667R00106